Man Who Ha[...]a account with almost o[...]hind Man Who Has It Al[...] *Who Has It All: A Patronizing Parody of Self-Help Books for Women*. *Flipping Patriarchy* is the first time the author writes in their own voice.

Twitter/X: @manwhohasitall
Facebook page: Man who has it all
Instagram: themanwhohasitall
Threads: manwhohasitall
Bluesky: @manwhohasitall.bsky.social
Shop: manwhohasitallshop.com

BY THE SAME AUTHOR

The Man Who Has It All: A Patronizing Parody of Self-Help Books for Women

FLIPPING
Patriarchy
Imagining a gender-swapped world

Man Who Has It All

MWHIA

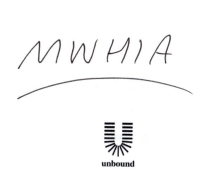

First published in 2025

Unbound
c/o TC Group, 6th Floor King's House, 9–10 Haymarket, London
SW1Y 4BP
www.unbound.com
All rights reserved

© Man Who Has It All, 2025

The right of Man Who Has It All to be identified as the author of this work has been asserted in accordance with Section 77 of the Copyright, Designs and Patents Act, 1988. No part of this publication may be copied, reproduced, stored in a retrieval system, or transmitted, in any form or by any means without the prior permission of the publisher, nor be otherwise circulated in any form of binding or cover other than that in which it is published and without a similar condition being imposed on the subsequent purchaser.

While every effort has been made to trace the owners of copyright material reproduced herein, the publisher would like to apologise for any omissions and will be pleased to incorporate missing acknowledgements in any further editions.

Text design by Ellipsis, Glasgow

A CIP record for this book is available from the British Library

ISBN 978-1-80018-367-4 (paperback)
ISBN 978-1-80018-368-1 (ebook)

Printed in Great Britain by Clays Ltd, Elcograf S.p.A.

1 3 5 7 9 8 6 4 2

This book is for anyone who can take a joke. It is not for the humourless, oversensitive or easily offended.

It is also dedicated to my fans and to myself. Together we have created a monster. Well done everyone.

Contents

Foreword	ix
Introduction	1
1. Nice Women	9
2. Dad's To-do List	27
3. Not Just a Pretty Beard	65
4. Heard the One About a Man Trying to Park a Car?	99
5. Men in Sport	125
6. Mister Chairwoman	147
7. Men's History	183
8. The Clitionary	199
Afterword	223
Acknowledgements	229
Further Reading	231
Inspired By	247
Notes	251
Supporters	259

Foreword

'So it's just one joke?' my dad asked in 2015 as he tried to understand my Twitter account. 'You reverse things said about women and say them about men instead? And that's it? Don't you think you'll run out of material?'

Run out of material? I thought. *RUN OUT OF MATERIAL? Are you for fucking real?* I didn't reply. Instead, I thought about the phrase 'lived experience' and how the material comes from a lifetime of conditioning, decades of noticing things and the first-hand experience of being a woman. I wanted to answer his question seriously. But how do you explain a lifetime?

Fast forward nearly ten years and the answer is still a hard no, I will not run out of material. I knew then, and I know now, that running out of material is unlikely to be a problem. Indeed, as my dad would find out later, he himself is a source of material. I remember him telling me when I was a child that women couldn't be funny because, in his view, Victoria Wood wasn't funny. I wondered what this meant for me, as a girl. Could I be funny?

Flipping Patriarchy

Nearly one million followers later and I know the answer. I am a satirist, a legend and a genius. As funny as fuck. And yes, I absolutely do say so myself. These words are rarely used to describe women, so I'll start as I mean to go on by flipping the language used to describe women and men. In the social media world, as if there is any other, the switcheroo is the content. This is what you are here for. Just one joke.

Two fucks in and you might be wondering if the swearing means I'm angry. The good news is I am. Good news because anger is the fuel that keeps the memes coming. It turns out that ridiculing the patriarchy is a more effective therapy than going on a spa day. The legitimate anger caused by the system of male oppression cannot be soothed by wellness products alone. Even the active skincare ingredients vitamin A and retinol are not effective enough to tackle structural inequalities.

In, or more accurately, *under* the patriarchy, who am I? More importantly, what do I look like? As a teenager, I learned from magazines that I could be reduced to a body shape, a skin type and a star sign. Pear-shaped, combination and Capricorn, thanks for asking. In the spring, my priority should be becoming 'Beach Body Ready', laughing alone with salad, investing in transitional pieces and spring cleaning. In the summer, I have sun-kissed, beachy waves and healthy, dewy skin (SPF of at least 50) with minimal make-up to avoid clogging my pores. In the autumn, I have auburn hair and freckles to match my cosy interior. In November, I look cute in a cream cable-knit jumper, cupping my hot chocolate with both hands. In December, I turn into the perfect host with party hair and a sparkly dress. Over Christmas I clog my face with make-up and eat rich festive food, ready for the new-year detox.

Slogans on women's clothes remind me to be lovely, happy and sparkly all year round. If I'm not wearing a slogan T-shirt, I can look to my water bottle for a helpful reminder to stay positive and always be kind, regardless of the context.

In the language of porn, I was a teen, progressed to a curvy blonde, became a MILF and, now that I am over twenty-five, an older woman. I also qualify as one of the F's in an FFM threesome porn video. Given the choice, which I assume feminism now grants me, I choose to be the F on the far left of the acronym, away from the thrusting M. Less optimistically, I am reduced to a moist, fuckable hole, god forbid a dry one. I'd need a vaginal moisturiser for that.

As a mother, regardless of whether or not men would like to fuck me (please no, I haven't got the time), I am also a type: a working mother, an earth mother or a tiger mum. Being a mum, followed closely by my marital status, weight, age and appearance (a simple yes or no answer to the question 'would you?'), is now my main identifier. This identity has been allocated to me; I have not chosen it from a drop-down menu. Unfortunately, as a woman, you cannot select 'default human' or 'standard person'. It is not on the list. Computer and patriarchy say no.

But what about my multidimensional personality? At best I could be bubbly, caring or nice. Realistically, as a busy mum of three, I am limited to uptight or bitter, ideally both.

Never complex or funny and certainly not a total legend. These words are ring-fenced and sacred, used only for boys and men. Even if I moved beyond my status as a blonde, or my dress size, I would always be a female something: a female scientist, a lady golfer or quite funny for a woman. Whatever my shape, whatever my hair type (think straw, flyaways) and whatever is going on inside my head, I should spend more of my precious time on this earth buying stuff to conceal it, improve it and make it acceptable. An actual life's work.

Which brings me on to this book and the writing of it. My prose is staccato. I am direct in places. This is because I am busy and don't have time for joining words. I am overwhelmed by the actual mental and emotional load, my day job, parenting and the never-ending work of remaining fuckable as I approach midlife. Satirising this experience is another task on my to-do list. @manwhohasitall adds another dimension, a meta-layer of pain, hypocrisy and laughs. It's one way to cope with the shit. As Jean-Paul Sartre wrote, I am half victim, half accomplice, like everyone else.[1]

Returning to my dad, what a gift he gave me. His era-appropriate sexism, backed up and reinforced by the media, TV and the workplace, prompted me to develop a secret snarl and an unhealthy cynicism about our gendered world into adulthood. Smiling on the outside through my twenties, I was storing it all up, building up a bank of injustices, biases, comments and other THAT'S NOT FAIR moments that I now use as material. So a genuine thank you to my dad for this early gift, but also for modelling how to be a

Foreword

contrarian and how to play devil's advocate, two of his favourite games. He can be proud that I take after him, using the same games to create a topsy-turvy world; one where I ask the question 'Can men be funny?'

Which reminds me of this helpful contribution from a knob on Twitter:

'This "person's" account is simply in existence to push a "man-hating" agenda dressed up as satire.' Man on Twitter

Erm . . . no, actually. I have two sons, a partner, a dad and three brothers. Some of my best friends are men. I adore men. How could I possibly hate men? The only thing this person hates is the patriarchy. Flipping it, and putting the shoe on the other foot, tells us why.

Introduction

@manwhohasitall is a social media account that exposes sexist bullshit. I imagine a world where men face the same kind of pressures as women, as Caitlin Moran writes about in *How To Be a Woman*:

> I have a rule of thumb that allows me to judge – when time is pressing, and one needs to make a snap judgment – whether some sexist bullshit is afoot. Obviously, it's not 100 per cent infallible but, by and large, it definitely points you in the right direction.
>
> And it's asking this question: 'Are the men doing it? Are the men worrying about this as well? Is this taking up the men's time? Are the men told not to do this, as it's "letting the side down"? Are the men having to write bloody books about this exasperating […] time-wasting bullshit?'
>
> Almost always the answer is: 'No. The boys are not being told they have to be a certain way. They are just getting on with stuff.'

In this fictional, gender-flipped world, it is the men who are doing it and worrying about it, and it is taking up their time. Meanwhile, women are not being told they have to be a certain way; we are the ones just getting on with stuff. @manwhohasitall is one big thought experiment rather than a manifesto or utopia. The intention is to make you think. I flip the patriarchy, put the shoe on the other foot, subvert the stereotypes, replace he with she, swapping man for woman, adding a little exaggeration along the way for laughs. It's like ChatGPT with knobs on. I am the knobs.

Back in the real world, I am of course just another woman having to write bloody books about 'this exasperating, time-wasting bullshit'. So why bother? I started writing @manwhohasitall on Twitter in 2015 because my enormous brain was full of feminism and creativity but I had nowhere to put it. Attempts at challenging sexist behaviour or starting discussions about gender stereotypes with family, friends or colleagues were quickly shut down, so I learned not to bother. The pushbacks 'not all men', 'misandry' or 'women can be violent too', delivered by an angry mansplainer, were enough to shut me up and put me back in my box. Part of me believed them when they said I was the problem, had an axe to grind, a chip on my shoulder and made everything about gender. But the other, braver, contrarian part of me wanted to prove them wrong. This motivation, combined with an interest in language and a healthy female ego, spurred me on. I set up the @manwhohasitall handle on Twitter, partly inspired by Caitlin Moran's questions above, but also by advertiser Paul Arden's business book *Whatever*

You Think, Think the Opposite. I took the title of the book as an instruction.

Out of my box, grinding my axe and making everything about gender turned out to be my happy place. @manwhohasitall became a safe and therapeutic outlet to get it all out. The reaction I got was validating. Encouraged by a rapid increase in followers, hundreds of retweets and comments from women in on the joke, I set up a Facebook page and later a satirical T-shirt shop and Instagram account.

The satirical T-shirts are popular, especially the matching Hers and His range which includes, for example, a standard Engineer T-shirt for women and a special, slightly more expensive Male Engineer version for men. A mum friend, who has no idea I am the writer behind @manwhohasitall, excitedly came to tell me in the playground about one of the boys' T-shirts in my shop that has the slogan 'Boys will be boys: kind, caring, thoughtful' printed on the front. She thought I would like it and she was right. It felt like the equivalent of what authors call, 'seeing my book out in the wild'. The satire was spreading beyond social media into the material world.

A follower summarises what you can expect to get from this book:

'You shake up my world and help me stay sane' Rachel, May 2023

So @manwhohasitall is a place of refuge and comedic relief, lessening the pain at the same time as making you laugh. But it is also a form of activism. In her academic study 'Satirical feminism and the Reparative Tweet: a discourse analysis of the gendered language of @manwhohasitall', Dr Katherine Rothschild, Lecturer in the Program for Writing and Rhetoric at Stanford University, coins the phrase 'reparative tweeting':

> The Twitter user @manwhohasitall addresses gendered language by using satire, tweeting from a fictional world where gender stereotypes are reversed [...] This study [...] identifies a model to humorously address and critique gendered language: Reparative Tweeting. This paper suggests that other forms of Reparative Tweeting or advocacy that relies on satire and community discourse may allow feminists to discuss gender bias without immediate pushback, and offer a model for showing, rather than telling, the story of gender discrimination.[1]

I like Dr Rothschild's idea of reparative tweeting; there is certainly plenty to reform and rectify in the patriarchal world of gender bias and discrimination. I also hope this book shows up things you may not have seen before that require repair: previously invisible hypocrisies, injustices, prejudices and falsehoods.

Most of what I expose and challenge through @manwhohasitall sits at the bottom of the rape culture pyramid, the kind of behaviour academics and campaigners classify as the foundation of men's violence against women and girls. The idea of the pyramid is that male violence is a continuum, with widespread attitudes and beliefs such as 'boys will be boys', sexist jokes, locker room banter and unequal pay reinforcing and excusing the male violence at the top of the pyramid.

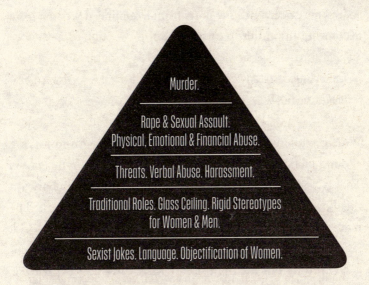

This is why @manwhohasitall matters. The account and its followers are chipping away at the lower half of the continuum, one post and one comment at a time.

As Felicity, a supporter of this book, says:

I want to tell you how much I appreciate your work. It teaches me about the horrors of the patriarchy in such a lovely way. Without you, I don't think I would have understood just how much the patriarchy ruins.

In turn, I would like to thank all my followers for teaching *me* through their comments, supporting this book and creating a community. My fans are often credited for being even funnier, smarter and more creative than the legend herself behind the account. As one Facebook follower points out, the comments underneath my posts from like-minded women have become an important part of the satire:

I always suggest reading the comments. The account is good, but the replies are GOLD.

Which, while I am in modest mode, brings me on to talking about qualifications, apologies and the limitations of this book. This is a short section, because there are none. I embark on this book with the confidence of a mediocre white man. The material comes from reversing what I see in the real world. So if you don't like it, don't blame me; I am just the messenger, churning out the opposite of what I live and experience. Blame the real world. End of. Think of me as like a spiritualist medium, an invisible go-between in a séance, channelling between two different worlds, the patriarchal and the satirical. Or, if that sounds like bollocks, 'one big moan' or 'passive-aggressive diatribe' will do.

Talking of diatribe, the experience of reading @manwhohasitall in long-form writing can be a bit much. Even my own internal monologue tells me to give it a rest. For this reason, I recommend you read this book in short bursts to feel the benefit. The constant reversal (here she goes again) is tedious, repetitive and irritating at times. It can also feel unfair, unsettling and unsavoury. However, this does reflect the actual experience of women; most of us hear and experience the same old sexist shit again and again. So proceed with caution, remember this is satire and take your time.

Now brave enough to step out of my box, and with a

Introduction

platform I deserve, I would like to answer the question about why I make everything about gender. My answer is that patriarchy started it. You told me women couldn't be funny, that girls can't do maths and that I had a lady brain. Until you put barriers in my way, I thought I could be anything. It was you, patriarchy (pokes finger at social system of dominance and privilege), who made everything about gender, making a giant fuss if I stepped out of line. So to return to the playground and to childhood, where a lot of this stuff starts, you did it first. You were the first one to bring it up. You raised the stink. You genderised me. And it's you who keeps going on about it. I wouldn't have even thought about gender if you hadn't mentioned it. So don't come crying to me if you don't like it. He who smelt it dealt it.

1.

Nice Women

Cubs Man is the story of my peak kind moment. I attended a Cubs meeting as a volunteer one evening, shamed into signing up as a helper by a visible rota on the wall, with parents encouraged to write their name against a session. I thought, while I'm here, I might as well make the most of it, play the games and get stuck in. One of the two Cub leaders asked us all to stand in a circle, ten or so children, including my daughter and her friend (Cubs is made up of girls and boys aged between eight and ten and a half years of age). I happened to be standing next to the other Cub leader, an adult man perhaps in his forties; an earnest, enthusiastic-seeming individual with a flushed face. Having arranged ourselves in a circle, we were then asked to hold hands. My daughter and her friend both watched me, sniggering, wondering what I would do. Would I quickly find a child to stand between me and the adult male to avoid having to hold his hand? Or would that look like I was trying to avoid holding his hand (which was exactly what I was trying to do)? How would that make him feel? Would he be offended?

Might he do something to try to avoid holding *my* hand? Or perhaps the other Cub leader would notice and ask us to shuffle around? Or maybe it didn't matter, just two people holding hands, nothing to see, no big deal. It was this thought, that it was all fine and normal, and something in the back of my mind about modelling confidence to my daughter, that made me suddenly reach out and take his hand in mine. There was no going back. Behaviour modelled, but what exactly was I teaching her? By mistake, I showed her that if in doubt, be polite. Don't make a fuss, just be nice. As I stood there, holding this man's big, damp hand, someone I had barely spoken to, I then felt unable to drop it. The instructions from the Cub leader kept coming, with no imminent sign of the activity requiring hand-holding actually taking place. It was only after most of the children had dropped hands, realising there was no point, that I felt able to wriggle my own hand free from his. Not once did it occur to me in that moment that I could actually have boundaries, and that choosing who I hold hands with could be one of them.

Cat Person

On the way home from Cubs, I thought about the viral story 'Cat Person', written by Kristen Roupenian and published in the *New Yorker*. The central character, Margot, decides to end a relationship with her older boyfriend, Robert, but she isn't sure how to do it politely but firmly. She eventually ends it abruptly in a text after advice from her roommate. When she sees him at a bar a month later, she worries that he is looking for her and she avoids him. That night, he sends a flurry of

Nice Women

text messages. At first his communications are friendly, but become more unpleasant and jealous when Margot does not reply. The story ends with him calling her 'Whore'.

While I would have been surprised if the volunteer Cub leader had called me a whore for dropping his hand in a circle of ten children, I faced the same uncertainty and pressure as Margot did: how to be polite but firm. Cat Person, unlike Cubs Man, is a breathtakingly resonant and, in places, grimly funny account of a woman's-eye view of a romantic relationship. The honesty of Margot's inner monologue throughout the story is part of the literary magic, because we learn that she prioritises Robert's feelings and perspective throughout, at the expense of her own. So while the story is told from Margot's point of view, we actually read it from two perspectives; the first is what she is really thinking (she doesn't particularly like him) and the second is what she imagines Robert is thinking (that he finds her young and hot). And that fantasy – his imagined consumption of her – matters more to her than what she actually wants. Margot is experiencing reality vicariously through what she believes he expects from her. The fact that she is smarter, younger and more attractive than him, thinks him ridiculous and doesn't even fancy him, is irrelevant.

Margot sat on the bed while Robert took off his shirt and unbuckled his pants, pulling them down to his ankles before realizing that he was still wearing his shoes and bending over to untie them. Looking at him like that, so awkwardly bent, his belly thick and soft and covered with hair, Margot recoiled.

But the thought of what it would take to stop what she had set in motion was overwhelming; it would require an amount of tact and gentleness that she felt was impossible to summon.[1]

We all have our own Cat Person or Cubs Man story where we prioritise men's feelings over our own comfort or safety, where we tie ourselves in knots to be tactful and gentle. Or perhaps we have many. I could fill a book of my own: Cinema Man, Radio 4 Man, Fountain Man, Train Man, Train Man 2, Porn Man, Retro Man, Conference Man, Antiques Man, Car Man. The thing these stories, which I am too embarrassed to tell, all have in common is the desperate need to be seen as nice, combined with the often secondary instinct to stay safe. We consider men's feelings before our own, hardly believing we are allowed, or worthy of, boundaries.

Just be kind

So we are taught to just be kind; it costs you nothing. In a world where you can be anything, be kind. Choose kindness. Throw kindness around like confetti! Think kind. Be kind. Stay kind. Kindness is beautiful. Dress yourself with kindness. If you can't be kind, be quiet.

Walk into many high-street clothes shops and you'll see these messages printed on products marketed to women and girls: T-shirts, pyjamas, water bottles, notebooks, jewellery, candles, pin badges, art prints, stationery, bags and more. The font is whimsical and in italics, the exhortations surrounded by jaunty butterflies, rainbows and flowers. You could literally dress yourself in kindness from head to toe,

Nice Women

from wearing a Kindness Matters headband in your hair to Choose Kindness sloganed trainers on your feet, completing the ensemble with a spritz of Kindness perfume and an Always Be Kind water bottle in your hand. Look kind, drink kind and smell kind. Staying kind overnight is easy too, in your Be Kind slipper socks, pyjamas and eye mask. On the inside, choose to think kind thoughts, day and night.

So just be kind. It's as simple as that. How nice. Who could argue with a kinder world?

Me actually. Because you do not see the same instruction printed on products designed for men and boys. If you think I am exaggerating, see Kate Long's (@volewriter) brilliant Twitter threads for heaps of evidence on the different messages printed on clothes aimed at women and men. This marked difference tells us that the kindness directive found on clothes for women and girls is not about being kinder to the planet, or that people should be kinder in general. There is something political about it, something larger at stake that does cost somebody something. These slogans are about a specific type of kindness, expected of women and girls. It is apparently women and girls who need to be more generous, considerate and self-sacrificing! Yes, that's right, because we aren't kind or caring enough already? I call this the kindness load, sister of the mental load, emotional load and feminist load: another form of never-ending, thankless, invisible labour. Kindness, although hidden in the apparently gender-neutral slogans, is women's work. By stealth, the slogan T-shirts become wearable oppression, an on-brand reminder for women and girls to prioritise others. And by others, I mean men.

Francesca Mallen, lead campaigner at Let Clothes Be

Clothes, a campaign to end gender stereotyping in the design and marketing of childrenswear, agrees:

> No, it's not just a T-shirt – and those are not just words. These sorts of slogans both reflect and reinforce the worst of us – boys are wild, troublesome; 'boys will be boys', right? Opposite girls who are constantly told their only worth lies in 'love' or being pretty.[2]

The 'just' in the 'just be kind' message is the interesting part. The 'just' implies it is simply, and only, a matter of being kind; no more complicated than that. It is not hard. And remember, in a world where you can be anything, you can choose kindness. If only it were that simple. If only we lived in a context-free world without history, power or oppression. In reality, we live in a world where too many women endure male violence, where women shoulder the majority of the care burden and where women already carry the majority of the mental and emotional load in relationships. Women don't choose this shit; it is chosen for us. We are socialised to be kind and polite and to sacrifice our time and resources at every turn. It is in this unequal context of care and sacrifice that the 'just be kind' mantra is delivered and aimed at the already-kind half of the population. Choosing to be kinder still is not only unwise and unhealthy, it is also exhausting. The reverse is actually true: we are often kind and polite by necessity to keep ourselves safe, because the alternative, which is to express our needs at a personal or collective level, can be dangerous. This is no choice at all. In this context, kindness is ugly.

It is easy to tell women and girls to be kind. Speaking the words, typing slogans instructing others to be kind and wearing a printed hoodie costs nothing. Actual daily self-sacrifice, thinking about other people's feelings and actively caring for others, in all its mundane, messy and invisible detail, does have a cost. It is about driving your mother-in-law to hospital, wiping your elderly dad's arse, organising a retirement card for a colleague at work, because otherwise none of this stuff gets done. This everyday caring work is what women already do, so to be told to be kind, from whatever source, is galling. Like being told to shut up, to get back in the kitchen or to calm down, the kindness instruction serves as another way of keeping us in our place. Because remember, if you can't be kind, be quiet.

Women are kind enough

My response to the 'be kind' mandate is that it can fuck right off. I have enough to do at home without being responsible for other people's smiles. I certainly do not want to smell kind. I dread to think what or who the scent of self-sacrifice might attract. Certainly nothing good. Being kind does, by definition, cost you something: it costs mental energy and time. It can cost you yourself. In a fantasy non-patriarchal world where I could indeed choose to be anything, being kind might be up there, alongside being courageous and authentic. But in this world, the one we actually live in, I am kind enough already thanks. If anything, and if I could actually choose, I would choose for women and girls to receive, not give, a shitload more kindness.

Love, love, love

Also under the umbrella of bullshit comes the diktat to love. Give love, spread love, radiate love, choose love. I have seen the word love printed three times on the same T-shirt, I assume to avoid doubt about what we are supposed to prioritise. And again, this is not a gender-neutral message. With some exceptions, the word love is printed on products aimed at women and girls. Love is apparently Our Thing. As Adrienne Rich says in her poem 'Translations' on the topic of verse written by women, love is our subject. It is what we talk about, write about and think about, and what we do. Love, it seems, is also women's work.

And now we are literally wearing it around our necks (love slogan necklace), on our bodies (LOVE LOVE LOVE T-shirt) and through our ears (love stud earrings). It would be ridiculous to argue we need a little less love in the world. But does it really all have to come from half of the population? I, for one, am willing to hang back on this one, remove it from my ankles and let someone else have a turn, freeing me up to train for a marathon, sit on the toilet in peace for a good half an hour or have a long afternoon nap. There is even a popular book by Robin Norwood called *Women Who Love Too Much*, presumably on the same shelf as Anne Wilson Schaef's *Meditations for Women Who Do Too Much* and Susan Nolen-Hoeksema's *Women Who Think Too Much* (the common message here is simply that women are Too Much). Note that it is the woman's responsibility to sort out this loving too much, thinking too much and doing too much problem, and definitely no one else's.

Related to the instruction to love and be kind are messages about being happy, positive, smiley and sparkly. Taken together, all of this sentimental crap amounts to our clothes gaslighting us. We might be giving out positive, happy vibes on the outside, but we could be feeling quite the opposite on the inside. Where is the space for women and girls to be unkind, angry, dull, negative and sad? Why do we have to be positive all the time? Do we have to spend every waking hour nurturing others with a perma-smile?

Here comes trouble

While women and girls are told to be kind, loving and happy, the messages on clothes for men and boys tell a different story. The exhortations are about breaking rules, digging dirt, causing trouble and being the boss. Boys can be complex human beings who get to do stuff; they can be geniuses, legends and heroes. Far from self-sacrifice, the slogans encourage men and boys to do their own thing, ignore others and make their own way. As women are told to give, give, give, men are told to take, take, take. As girls are told to sparkle, boys are told to make a mess. As boys are taught to be bad, girls are taught to be nice. As T-shirts for men are printed with slogans such as 'Destroy Boundaries', T-shirts for women bear the message 'No Boundaries'. And all this is reinforced by the maxim 'boys will be boys'. I prefer the harder to remember and less popular maxim 'boys will be what we encourage them to be, expect them to be and tell them to be'. I never had a 'genius' slogan T-shirt, but I didn't need one to work this out.

Nice men

And so it comes as no surprise that the bar for a man to be considered 'nice' is very, very low. As long as he isn't obviously violent or sexist, he is assumed to be a decent bloke . . . The same low bar applies to being a good dad or a family man. Simply living in the same house as his children appears to be enough for a dad to qualify for the title, regardless of his actual, material contribution. There is an exception: a dad who leaves his family entirely and chooses not to be 'involved' in his child's life. He is called an absent father. But note, the value-neutral and merely descriptive 'absent'. Not a bad father. In fact, the bar is so low to be considered a good dad that even a man who murders his wife, mother-in-law, five children then himself is memorialised in an obituary as a 'loving father'.[3] News reports about men who murder their wives and kids often quote shocked neighbours describing the murderer as a 'devoted father' or 'a really nice man'.[4]

Turning the tables

Imagine a topsy-turvy world, where the definition of a nice woman centres on one who doesn't beat her husband and lets her man wear what he wants. She would be called a really good woman, with a heart of gold.

There is a poem about this called 'Nice Men' written by Dorothy Byrne. Her work expertly ridicules the incredibly low bar we have for a man to be considered nice, for example a nice man gives his wife freedom over how to spend her time, helps his wife around the house and *actually* likes women better than men (but only because they listen and are understanding). She also praises nice men at work who manage not to shout at women for getting things wrong and says how nice it is when men tell their wives not to get so worked up about things. Her gentle understatement in the poem adds to the pathos. I love it.

I often write about a fictional character Claire, CEO, on-line. She is also a nice woman. She has friends and some of them are really nice too. Let's hear from Claire and her mates, who exist in a parallel universe, and find out what makes them tick.

'Having a son has taught me how to respect men.' Claire, CEO

When a woman has a son, something unexpected happens. She realises something quite profound: that men are worthy of respect. Although for some women, one son isn't enough:

'It wasn't till I'd had my third son that I finally realised men are people, too.' Shalini, MP

You got there in the end, Shalini; some women never do, so well done. Owning a son or a husband really brings it home:

'The first time I held my son, I knew from the bottom of my heart that he was human. Still not sure about the ones I'm not related to, though.' Hanneke, barrister

Heartwarming – this shows just how far women have come. However, some women still struggle to make the leap from recognising men as equal human beings to allowing a man to speak for himself, despite being surrounded by strong, independent men:

'I have a father, brother, husband, son, uncle, nephew and two grand-fathers! That shows I am an expert in men and can speak for them.' Jasmin, director

This leaves women with no sons in a difficult position:

'As a woman with no sons, I find it hard to respect men.' Tasha, engineer and mother of no sons

So does this mean that women like Tasha must rely on mere speculation that men have experiences and lives worth respecting? Some people might think Tasha should somehow automatically respect men, but can we really blame her for this entirely pragmatic stance? Because don't forget, woman is a rational creature, unlikely to be influenced by what cannot be proven. One of my Facebook followers agreed:

Quite right, respect must be earned. I have a serious suggestion – neutral woman scientists should conduct clinical trials to find out objectively whether men are worthy of respect.

Although many would argue clinical tests aren't necessary, at least these women are making an effort to understand the male creature. The cavewomen types on Twitter won't even try to get it:

Happily for me I only have a daughter, so I'm at liberty not to respect men. Thank goodness for that!

This disappointing attitude is why we need good role models like Claire, CEO, who are prepared to show their softer side in public. Claire says that even before her son was born, she believed deep down that men are just as equal as women. As a young woman, she didn't indulge in non-consensual penis-grabbing even though she had the opportunity and could have got away with it. How many other women would be so woke?

Claire grew up with a great role model. Her mother never beat her father, even though he was provocative, constantly nagging about the cooking, cleaning, washing and ironing. Indeed, she grew up surrounded by feisty men – her father, uncles and brothers all had careers in their own right.

Respecting men doesn't mean you can't still open doors for them, as Kenzie and Georgina demonstrate:

'I always open the car door for my man to make him feel weak, useless and controlled. He loves it.' Kenzie, MP

At least she's being honest.

'I always say "gentlemen first" because gentlemen are precious, delicate creatures who need a guiding hand and I also like to look at their lovely bottoms.' Georgina, lawyer

I'm confident that Claire, Kenzie, Georgina and the crew wouldn't dream of degrading a young man without asking him first. You meet good women from across the political spectrum who respect men, even if they show it in different ways. Left-wing women tend to use their male friends (known as male allies) and clever intellectual writing to prove how nice they are. Right-wing women demonstrate their respect in other ways, such as telling men to smile and putting them on a pedestal. There are some nice women out there, if you know where to look.

However, not all women are as quick to join the modern world. As Claire says:

> *We're in a different time. Men didn't used to be people. It's taking time to adjust. Bear with us during this difficult period.*

And men must understand this. It takes time for women to realise that the world has moved on, and it's no longer okay to treat men as objects. So this is absolutely where our focus must be: sympathy with the women who have to adjust to the new world. The real victims in all this; confused and bewildered about what they are and are not allowed to do anymore. After all, if men want true equality, they have to bring women along with them. It's no good being angry and putting women off by mentioning all the bad things. If men want to change the world, they should be kind, positive and nice.

Here are some rules for a lady to live by, inspired by similar rules for gentlemen that I found online. You can see a list of websites in the Inspired By section at the back.

The Lady's Code of Conduct

A lady respects all men. Regardless of who they are, she uses dignity and thoughtfulness when speaking to a gentleman.

A lady takes care to groom herself. She uses soap, shampoo and deodorant.

A lady is never late and arrives at least ten minutes early to greet her date. If a lady must cancel, she first informs the gentleman and graciously commits to make up for it another time.

A lady always lets a gentleman go first. She opens the door for him, lets him order his food before her at a restaurant and will allow him to pull out in front of her car.

You can trust a lady. Regardless of the time or location, she will always respect a gentleman's boundaries and make him feel safe.

When walking on a pavement together, a lady lets her gentleman walk on the inside, away from the traffic. She protects him.

A true lady does not prey on a man. She never exploits her man or takes advantage of his caring nature.

A lady will never take her man for granted and always remembers to value him. She will reassure him of his worth regularly with pleasant words.

A lady flatters her man and remembers to remark upon his good looks.

A man likes to be surprised. A real lady buys her man unexpected and thoughtful gifts and sends him letters.

A lady does not lie. Keeping her word is of utmost importance to her and is the true mark of a lady.

A lady does not silence her man or talk over him. She listens with great interest to all the things he has to say.

Realising when to back down and say sorry is a quality possessed by a lady. A lady is prepared to acknowledge when she has done wrong.

When provoked, a lady resists the temptation to use her fists. A true lady never hits a man.

A lady will always make way for a gentleman, a child or the elderly. She will not stand and watch a gentleman carry a heavy bag.

A lady tunes into the true nature of her man, his unique foibles and fancies.

When a true lady settles down with a nice young boy, she becomes a family woman.

A family woman

A family woman is an active, hands-on mum who is involved in her child's life. She remembers her children's birthdays, changes nappies when they are babies and even takes the kids to the park at the weekend! She makes a point of spending time with each of her children.

In an alternative dictionary, a family woman might be defined as: a woman with a husband (or who lives with their partner) and children, who particularly enjoys spending time at home.

She may or may not help with the housework, play with the kids much or be at home every night of the week. But who cares? At least she stuck around. A family woman always comes home to her husband and kids, and that's all that matters.

The low bar

If the bar for men is ridiculously low to be considered nice, kind or a perfect family man, and the bar for women is way too high, what new wearables could be marketed to redress this imbalance?

Imagine walking into a real-life department store in a town or city near you, heading for menswear and seeing men's shirts with the slogan 'think kind thoughts' printed on the collar, men's underpants with little reminders to be kind embroidered on the crotch and men's sunglasses with instructions to smile etched into the arms. Move to men's accessories and find laptop bags telling men to stay positive, phone cases instructing men to sparkle with joy and water bottles reminding men to only think happy thoughts. He could dress himself in kindness and love from head to toe, from the Born to Sparkle cap on his head, to the I Eat Glitter for Breakfast socks on his feet. He could complete the look with a splash of Kindness is Handsome aftershave and keep himself fully hydrated with his Kindness Forever water bottle. Look kind, drink kind and smell kind.

As you walk out of the shop, you admire a smiling dad with a pretty beard holding hands with his two sons. All of them are wearing Love, Love, Love T-shirts with matching caps, the design enhanced with hearts, flowers and unicorns. That's eighteen loves altogether. Enough to change the world? The woman following behind, possibly the mother, is engrossed in her phone. She wears a plain hoody and jeans.

Imagine on the table in front of you in the bookshop next door, three non-fiction bestsellers on a three-for-two offer: *Men Who Do Too Much*, *Men Who Think Too Much* and *Men Who Love Too Much*. Buy all three and get a free 'Always Be Handsome' bookmark.

Would this be such a bad thing? Imagine a world where all men chose to be kind every day and stayed that way. So, all men, just be kind. It is as simple as that. It costs you nothing. Who could argue with a kinder world?

The Kindness Load

- Be kind always
- Be polite
- Be nice
- Be quiet
- And don't forget to smile!

2.

Dad's To-do List

'Do we have any waterproof plasters?' Claire shouts to her husband, Liam. Liam doesn't answer her because he's livid. Why doesn't Claire know if they have any waterproof plasters? Why is he responsible for knowing literally EVERYTHING in this house? Doesn't she realise he's trying to do a million things at once in the kitchen? Liam just wishes his wife would take some responsibility.

After several minutes, Liam removes the pan from the heat and walks upstairs briskly, picking up a pile of things from the bottom step as he goes. On the landing, with his spare hand, he stoops down to gather up a phone charger, a dirty sock, a damp swimming costume and a corn on the cob. Liam puts everything in a washing basket to take upstairs but keeps hold of the sweetcorn. He finds Claire in the bathroom relaxing on a chair, phone in hand, waiting for him. Their youngest child is sitting in the bath holding out a finger with a tiny cut waiting for Liam to arrive to make it better. Already, age four, she knows that Daddy is the only person in the house who can do anything.

Liam reaches just above Claire's head, opens the bathroom cabinet, locates the waterproof plasters immediately and places them on her lap. Claire yawns and tells Liam how tired she is without looking up from her phone. Liam manages not to say anything sarcastic, silently congratulating himself for being the adult in the relationship. He tries to wedge the corn in the cob in the tiny bin under the sink but it's already full. He notices the bin lid is still broken, covered in something sticky, possibly pineapple. He pauses for a moment and imagines a different life, one without an active compost heap in the ensuite. After reminding Claire to remind their daughter to wash her hair and put a plaster on her finger, Liam cleans the bin lid with a wet wipe, making a mental note to bring a fresh bin bag back upstairs later. As he leaves the room, he remembers with a jolt that he still hasn't got a card and present for a child's birthday party in the morning or taken the wet laundry out of the washing machine. Everything, he thinks, as he fights back tears, is going to shit.

As Liam and the sweetcorn return to the kitchen, he mutters 'for fuck's sake' under his breath and thinks about everything he is responsible for. He feels overwhelmed. He starts to write a list of all the things he does and begins to feel angry. The phrase 'Why do I have to do everything, literally EVERYTHING?' goes round and round in his head. He tenses up as he imagines Claire asking him if he knows the meaning of the word literally. Before he has time to get even more annoyed, a reminder goes off on his phone: the plumber is due to arrive any minute to fix a dripping tap. At last, a job that's been on his to-do list for months might finally be ticked off. He found

Dad's To-do List

the plumber after a recommendation from a dad friend on a school WhatsApp group. Another thing I have to do, he thinks, wondering why his wife never joins any groups. Is it really because she's socially awkward as she claims, or is it because she can't be arsed? Liam remembers with a flash of resentment that he used to have the luxury of being socially awkward pre-kids. But not anymore. Liam's entire personality, it seems, has been sacrificed now he's a dad, while Claire remains unchanged, as if nothing had ever happened.

After turning the hob back on, grabbing a pile of clean dry clothes and a small bin bag, Liam rushes back upstairs to check that Claire and their daughter have finished in the ensuite so the plumber can do her job. They have moved on, but the floor is covered in water, the bath is still full and there's a sopping wet hoodie in the sink. He grabs a hand towel, stands on it and uses it to shuffle across the floor to get to the bath to avoid soaking his slippers. As he bends down to pick out a freshly opened, now soggy, soap blocking the plughole, Claire pops her head around the door to ask what's for tea. Liam empties the bath without answering, banging his head on the bathroom cabinet as he stands up. He momentarily wonders if he might have to go to A&E but quickly forgets when the doorbell rings. He's too busy for a head injury. Knowing no one else will answer the door, Liam rushes back downstairs to let the plumber in, making a mental note to tell his wife how useless she is later. Claire is left on the landing, apparently unable to accelerate or move quickly, except when she's competing in a triathlon or leaving the house for the pub. She lollops slowly downstairs, taking nothing with her as she

Flipping Patriarchy

goes, with a bewildered look on her face, oblivious to what's going on, in particular and also in general.

The plumber comes in cheerfully, walking straight past invisible Liam to shake the now authoritative Claire's hand, giving her a womanly grin. They go upstairs to talk about very important woman-things: taps, washers and faulty seals in the bathroom. Claire puts on a special woman voice when she's talking to a tradeswoman, which makes Liam laugh because she knows precisely fuck all about any of it. Leave them to it though, he thinks; at least that's one thing she can actually do. Finally, Liam can relax and can get on with dinner, after he's cuddled the little one who is crying because 'Mummy didn't put a plaster on.' Liam notices his daughter's hair is still dry, Claire forgot to wash it. He considers going on strike, and wonders how many days, weeks or months it would take before anyone noticed. How long would the wet towels stay on the floor? Who would answer the door? Would the beds ever be changed? Would the kids make it to school? What would they eat? Who would find the kitchen scissors? How long does it take for a dressing gown to rot? Would flies take control of the entire house? It's just easier to do it myself, he thinks, as the front door slams and Claire walks in relaxed, smiling and triumphant. 'Well, that's the tap sorted, then.'

That night, and in a slightly better mood after the kids have gone to bed, Liam thinks telling Claire how useless she is may not improve the situation, so he completes his list of EVERY-THING, all the invisible things he does to keep on top of the house and children. After finishing his own list, he writes down Claire's modest contribution and then types both lists into a spreadsheet, hoping that once she sees and compares the two lists, she will realise just how hard he works. He pictures her incredulous face, full of remorse, admiration and gratitude. For the first time, she will realise just how lucky she is. He imagines the newly humbled Claire becoming the ultimate hands-on mum as a result, powering through household chores, enthusiastically joining school WhatsApp groups and taking on more and more responsibility each day.

Unfortunately, it doesn't quite work out like that. When Claire begrudgingly looks at the spreadsheet after being reminded eight times, she argues with every point on his list, claiming that either it doesn't need doing or that she does it too. Claire explains to Liam that everything is in fact fine. She also reminds him how lucky he is because after all, some mums do a lot less than she does. After several hours of arguing about how many times Claire has made dinner, in total, since they have been together, Liam asks her if she would just try to take more responsibility. Claire says of course, just tell me what needs doing and I will do it.

Claire's jobs:
- A full-time job
- Bins: putting bins out and bringing bins in weekly
- Dishwasher: stacking and unloading daily
- Lightbulbs: replacing old with new
- DIY: indoor repair jobs, cutting the grass, trips to the tip
- Annual BBQ: cooking and serving meat
- Annual curry: cooking a curry for an occasion
- Babysitting: staying in to babysit the kids when asked

- Car: taking car for MOT
- Holidays: packing own case
- Christmas: getting tree down from the loft/buying real tree

Liam's jobs:

Work
- Works three days a week

Kids
- Planning activities for the weekend: playdates, parties, soft play, cinema
- Bedtime and mornings: putting little kids to bed, reminding older kids to go to bed
- Getting dressed and ready: laying clothes out the night before, making sure uniform and PE kit is washed and ready to wear
- Hygiene: bathing small children and making sure older ones wash, nailcare and haircuts
- Researching: kids' health, development and behaviour
- Helping out at extracurricular activities: e.g. Brownies, Cubs, football, dancing

School
- Organising drop-offs and pick-ups to and from school and out-of-school activities
- Researching schools and nurseries and applying for places
- School work: getting kids to do homework, revise for exams and practise instruments, checking school bags for letters
- Parents' evening: booking slots, attending, reminding Claire to attend

Dad's To-do List

- Managing the cash kids take to school: donations for charity days, tuck shop and bus money, as well as managing payments for activities; childcare vouchers/tax-free childcare, after-school club, swimming, etc.
- Dressing-up days: remembering the dates, making or buying costumes
- Deciding what to do with kids' artwork from school or nursery
- School trips: organising payment, volunteering to help out, buying clothes or equipment

Housework

- Daily cleaning: bathroom, toilet and kitchen
- Frequent cleaning: hoovering, floors, windows and mirrors, changing the toilet roll, picking up towels, coats and clothes off the floor (or getting Claire and the kids to do it themselves), cleaning mud off the carpet, sweeping up cat litter, wiping fingerprints off glass
- Spring cleaning: dusting cobwebs, washing curtains, upholstery, washing duvets and carpets
- Tidying: kids' toys, sorting out miscellaneous piles of kids' stuff, unpacking kids' bags
- Laundry: washing clothes, hanging washing out, ironing, putting clothes away, changing bed linen
- Occasional laundry: washing items such as dressing gowns, shower curtains and coats, hand-washing delicate items, taking clothes to dry cleaners
- Guest visits: tidying and cleaning before guests arrive and changing bed linen

Food

- Shopping: big food shop and top-up shops
- Meal planning: researching recipes, getting food out of the freezer, batch cooking
- Preparing meals: making packed lunches and healthy snacks, preparing breakfast for younger children, cooking evening meal, making weekend breakfast and lunches
- Tidying away after meal preparation and encouraging Claire and kids to do the same
- Knowing what everyone likes to eat and dietary requirements: kids, Claire, friends, relatives

Clothes/shoes

- New clothes: noticing when Claire and the kids need new clothes and buying them, knowing what size clothes Claire and the kids wear
- Managing old clothes: storing clothes for younger children/cousins/friends to grow into, selling or giving to charity
- Buying special kit: e.g. dancing, football, and sewing badges onto Brownies/Cubs uniform
- Cleaning shoes and boots

Home

- Home improvements: researching, decision-making, getting quotes, taking time off to let tradeswomen in, project-managing the work
- Home and garden furniture and decor: researching, decision-making and buying
- Home storage: deciding on a place for everything, encouraging Claire and kids to put things away

Dad's To-do List

- Home insurance: getting quotes, decision-making, renewal
- Decluttering: garage, cupboards and loft

Health

- Dentist, doctor and optician appointments: deciding who needs to go and when, booking for Claire and kids
- Everyday health: making sure kids brush their teeth, being aware of high temperature, rashes, headlice, skin conditions, allergies, etc.
- Illnesses: taking time off work at short notice when kids are ill, or asking Claire to
- Sun health: buying sunscreen and making sure everyone applies it
- Medicine: buying and administering it

Pets

- Walking the dog
- Feeding pets
- Cleaning out pets: litter trays, cages and hutches, etc.
- Booking vet appointments
- Hoovering up pet hair and cleaning up after accidents

Holidays

- Preparing for holidays: deciding where to go and when, family packing for holiday (everything except Claire's suitcase, which she does herself), sorting out pet care, window cleaners, etc. while away
- Post holiday: unpacking, laundry, paying for pet care, thanking neighbours, etc.
- Looking after neighbours' pets when they go on holiday
- School holidays: planning childcare and holiday clubs

Social

- Participating in WhatsApp groups: family, school, neighbourhood
- Organising social occasions with friends as a couple or family
- Organising date nights

Celebrations

- Birthdays: knowing when everyone's birthday is, buying and wrapping presents in advance, writing and sending/delivering cards, giving relatives present ideas for the kids, organising parties
- Other occasions: sending occasion cards to relatives: home/ job/ baby/retirement
- Present drawer: ensuring card and present drawer is stocked with emergency cards and gifts, Sellotape and wrapping paper
- Parties: replying to party/wedding invitations, organising who can attend, storing balloons, candles, tablecloths, decorations, etc.
- Leaving money out for the tooth fairy
- Easter: organising egg hunt, Easter crafts, buying Easter eggs, organising and preparing celebration meal
- Halloween: organising trick or treating and Halloween fancy dress
- Christmas: everything except getting the tree down from the loft/ buying real tree

Poor Claire

Claire and Liam feature in many of my social media posts about housework and childcare. When I post about their to-do lists, my Facebook feed lights up with people in on the joke. Followers take part in the comments, extend the joke, and have fun roleplaying with each other in a gender-flipped world. The injustice! Poor Claire. She works full time, brings home the bacon and *still* has to help Liam with the kids and housework? Liam needs to get a grip. He only works three days a week. What on earth does he do on his days off? He's lucky Claire helps him at all. Many posters are outraged that Claire has to stack the dishwasher when she's been at work all day. All women want is to come home from work to a happy husband and kids who are pleased to see her. Is that really too much to ask?

Unreasonable Liam

Most of my followers agree that not everything on Liam's list needs doing – he's making a meal of it. Can't he just get a cleaning gentleman to help him? Why is he still ironing? Why aren't his kids getting themselves out of bed? Why is 'storing balloons, candles and tablecloths' on the list? Isn't that a two-minute job? Typical man, making mountains out of molehills. If Claire added every little thing to her list, it would be as long as Liam's. She once made pancakes at the weekend, where is that on the list? And the most important job of all is missing – washing the car!

Still playing along, some women boast about how much they help their husbands. One woman is more than willing to go to the shop on her way home from work if asked, as long as he gives her the list and detailed instructions about what the items look like (photos perhaps?) and where she can find them. Another poster says all her husband has to do is ask for help, and she will gladly lend a hand (as long as he asks nicely!). The commentary continues with one woman not afraid to say what everyone else is thinking: that the tasks on Liam's list 'would

Flipping Patriarchy

feel demeaning'. She asks other women if they can really see themselves hanging washing out or cleaning a toilet? Imagine! How embarrassing! She follows with a tip for young married women out there – 'If you're persuaded to do the weekly shop, subtlety mess it up so you're never asked to go again!'

Liam can't win

After agreeing that Claire has far too much to do and Liam is making stuff up, my followers go on to discredit Liam's list further by saying his chores aren't really chores because a) he enjoys them, b) he is good at them, and c) he just happens to be better at them. This leaves everyone looking at the thread wondering what all the fuss is about. Does Liam simply enjoy nagging and complaining? Why is he so uptight? Can't he just chill out? Does he need therapy? Advice for Liam pours in as the praise for Claire continues.

The imaginary Liam starts to believe that maybe the commenters are right, he just needs to get a grip. Men, also in on the joke, chip in to say that Liam gives all men a bad name – if they can successfully juggle radiant skin, a gorgeous home, kids and a job, why can't he? Why did Liam have kids in the first place if he didn't want to look after them? Liam is defeated; everything is stacked against him and he can't win. He must put up and shut up, ideally with a lovely big smile on his face. After all, women like to see positive men!

Liam's mental load

Liam decides to have a break from Facebook and he reads a cartoon in the *Guardian* written by an angry middle-aged husband. He learns the meaning of the phrase 'mental load' and thinks about how much he holds in his head. It's not just the delivering or doing of the tasks, it's the thinking about them. Liam tries to explain the phrase 'mental load' to Claire, but she's defensive and responds by listing all the things she does: 'I put the kids to bed last night', and 'Don't forget I stack the dishwasher every day.'

So Liam writes about everything that's in his head and tries to capture the full extent of the mental load. It's not just the doing of the tasks, it's the thinking about them.

Researching everything

First comes researching everything, from choosing the best pushchair to how to get children to revise for their A levels. Liam is responsible for thinking about whether the middle child might have an allergy, the best way to get rid of ants, how to remove mould from the bath, which jabs you need to go on holiday and, at the time of writing, whether using an air fryer saves money.

Anticipating everything

Next is anticipating everything: anticipating that the oldest will need his own bedroom soon, anticipating that the middle one will come home from Cubs hungry, anticipating that the children will get bored at Grandad's house, anticipating that someone will need to take time off work to let the builder in and anticipating that it's time for the little one to start potty training.

Remembering everything

Once Liam has anticipated everything, it's his job to remember everything. For example, remembering what each child needs to take to school every day, remembering to remind Claire to put the bins out, remembering to take the laundry out of the washing machine, remembering to get the cat wormed, remembering how his father-in-law likes his coffee and remembering to add cling film to the big shop.

Noticing everything

To help Liam to remember everything, he has to notice everything. This includes noticing that the birthday cards are still on the mantelpiece from three weeks ago, noticing the floor wipes are running out, noticing that the little one's toenails need cutting, noticing that the bathroom sink needs cleaning, noticing that someone has left scissors in reach of the two-year-old and noticing that the oldest hasn't brushed his teeth for three days.

Deciding everything

A related burden for poor Liam is making decisions on everything to do with the house and children. For example, Liam decides what to throw away and what to keep in the fridge, decides what to make for dinner, decides where to go on holiday, decides what colour to paint the walls, decides which cot to buy, decides how old is too old for a dummy and decides whether the oldest child should be allowed to have a phone. Claire often reminds Liam how lucky he is to be able to make all these decisions, and jokes with a big smile on her face that he's 'the boss!' Liam isn't so lucky when he is blamed if the holiday turns into a disaster or the cot he chooses takes Claire nineteen days to assemble.

Knowing everything

Because Liam has been doing everything for so long, and certainly since the children were born, he knows everything. Liam knows where child number two's school shoes are located, knows what each child likes to eat, knows what the weather is like outside, knows where the passports are kept, knows what's in the fridge, knows what's for dinner when asked, knows how much they should spend on a child's friend's birthday present and knows what size clothes his children wear. Related to knowing everything, Liam also has to answer questions about everything, so if Claire texts 'Is this cheese still okay to eat?' while Liam is on a rare weekend away, Liam should stop whatever he is doing to answer. Because Liam knows everything.

Project managing everything

Liam has a lot to keep track of. It's his responsibility to check that Claire has remembered to pick up the little one from Grandma's house, chase the plumber for a quote, remember to praise the children when they do something well and check the use-by dates on food in the freezer. When Liam reminds Claire to do something, she says he's nagging her and calls him a control freak. Liam asks on Dadsnet whether Claire is right and if he is being unreasonable. The response is mixed: some say Liam should just chill out and others agree that he should go on strike and see if anyone notices.

Back in the real world

My posts about Claire and Liam are among my most popular because women see themselves as Liam: overwhelmed by responsibilities and unable to do much about it. Those commenting on the posts are painfully fluent on the impossible circumstances many women find themselves in. The posters know exactly how to pretend to silence Liam and keep him in his place, because they have heard the same directed at them. They choose words and phrases to describe Liam's behaviour carefully, such as 'whining', 'nagging' and 'should be grateful'. These accusations sound out of place and ridiculous when aimed at the fictional Liam because we are so used to hearing them used to refer to women. In the same vein, the questions my followers reflexively ask, like 'What does he do all day?' and 'Doesn't he know men in other countries have it worse?' are pitch perfect. We have heard it all before.

Reading Claire and Liam's list of tasks and the torrent of like-minded comments exposes the unequal division of labour in the home between many heterosexual couples. By putting the shoe on the other foot, it becomes painfully obvious that the typical set-up is ludicrously unfair and rigged in men's favour. The standard justifications for the status quo are similarly ridiculous when exposed through the satirical switcheroo.

But women were born to clean

The first and most dangerous explanation for inequality in the home is biological, as these satirical posts on Twitter highlight:

TODAY'S FACT: Thanks to neuroscience, we now know that women have a different 'cognitive retinal architecture' and can't actually see a washing machine.

Ever wondered why your wife 'can't iron'? Science has the answer! It's because men's brains are actually WIRED to see wrinkles in fabric.

TODAY'S QUESTION: Will scientists ever find out why men are naturally attracted to unpaid caring work?

'My wife says she doesn't know how to choose, buy or wrap presents. She says I have a natural talent for these things. I think she's right!'
Lewis, busy dad of three

Imagine if we believed that men were naturally attracted to caring work and the scientific research followed this hypothesis. What would studies looking at the male brain discover? How long would it take to find an evolutionary explanation for this behaviour? What would looking at the animal kingdom tell us about the male of the species and their love of housework? My guess is that with enough funding and political support, it wouldn't take long for evolutionary psychologists, neuroscientists and biologists to present a wealth of evidence suggesting that the male human does indeed have a natural gift for knowing when the bathroom needs cleaning. Taking it further, if the tabloids were run by women, might it serve their interests to publish this 'science' as news?

Notice the use of the word 'natural'. If we believed that it was a man's biological destiny to care and clean, then it suggests that nothing can be done. The appeal to nature as a rhetorical tactic is a powerful one; what is natural is shorthand for what is right and good. Who in their right mind would argue against nature?

In a similar vein, the imaginary chief executive Claire celebrates the wonderful male brain:

> *'I do envy the wonderful male brain – that innate natural ability to know when the bathroom needs cleaning, to look gorgeous and to make my dinner.'* Claire, CEO

The use of the word 'wonderful' is deliberate because the word suggests that women are mythical creatures with unknowable qualities. This framing suggests that there is no point attempting to understand the 'mysterious female brain' any further, as long as the cleaning gets done.

Women enjoy it

Another common belief is that women actually *enjoy* tidying up, making packed lunches and looking after children for long periods of time. If we are doing it and not complaining about it, then everything must be fine, as these tweets illustrate:

> *TODAY'S FACT: The truth of the matter is, men just don't WANT the top-paid jobs. They prefer laundry, cleaning and childcare. Leaving me to pursue my career uninterrupted.*

TODAY'S QUESTION: *Why oh why do men insist on cleaning the bathroom if they don't enjoy doing it? Makes no sense.*

'Men do the majority of unpaid cleaning and caring work because they really, really enjoy it. Their choice. Their fault. End of story.' Claire, CEO

When applied to men, how we laugh. It's obviously ridiculous; just because someone does something, it doesn't mean they enjoy it. Most of the time, it's as simple as a task needs to be done and someone has to do it. But the argument goes that for every woman who doesn't enjoy mopping the floor, there will be another who loves it. So where's the problem? No one should prevent women from having the freedom to do thankless, unpaid work in the home. Because that's the best kind of freedom, isn't it? The freedom to serve men and get little or no thanks, pay or reward for it.

Men are useless

TODAY'S FACT: *Science says women are useless and should spend all Christmas Day on the sofa drinking, watching TV and playing games.*

TODAY'S QUESTION: *Is your wife a big kid at heart too? Mine is. I tidy up after her and organise her life. Sometimes it feels like I have four kids, not three!*

'My wife says she doesn't know how to iron, use a washing machine or cook. She says I have a TALENT for these things. I think she's right.' Thomas, busy dad

Flipping Patriarchy

While women are apparently naturally gifted when it comes to housework and childcare, men are often affectionately considered to be useless, or, using more words, completely fucking useless. This collusion is reinforced by the way dads are addressed in marketing campaigns. Twitter handle @dad_marketing, an American dad, shares examples of adverts that ignore dads altogether and only refer to mums, and at best assume dad is a helper. One example from many on his blog is the company Playtex Baby, which features only one photo of a dad on its entire website and doesn't mention dads in any of its stories about bottles, nappies, dummies or cups.[1]

Returning to the satire, I pose the question on Twitter, *It is often claimed that women are simply 'useless' around the house. Is this really true?* One woman responds to say that yes, women are completely useless and that only last week she discovered that toilets aren't self-cleaning. Another goes with the biological explanation, suggesting it's because women just don't see things and wonders if it's genetic or perhaps poor eyesight.

Using these three popular justifications for inequality in parenting and in the home are effective ways to maintain the status quo. If women were born to clean, they enjoy it, and men are useless at it anyway, where's the problem? Indeed, what's YOUR problem? If you are an exception to this biological rule, then it's your job to do something about it. And regardless of the situation you find yourself in, if you are a woman, it is definitely your fault.

It's your fault

Working husband and father? Feeling overwhelmed? YOUR FAULT. Bake lighter pastry, talk less and learn to SMILE.

You will feel much more relaxed if you turn that frown upside down!

Working husband and father? Feeling overwhelmed? YOUR FAULT. Drink more water, get up earlier and dress in your 'wow' colours.

If it is your fault, it is your responsibility to find a solution.

Working dad? If you struggle to get your wife to do her share of the housework, why not write a chore list and give her tasks she enjoys?

And how lucky you are if your husband helps you with *your* jobs!

'My wife is actually really good. She hangs up her clothes and even irons her own tops.' Carlos, age thirty-seven

You're a very lucky man, Carlos.

THREE CHEERS for women who willingly give up their own free time to help their husbands with the cleaning.

Especially when they could be catching up on work, going to the gym or relaxing in the pub.

'My wife actively participates in the care of our children. She even volunteers to give them a bath or put them to bed on her own sometimes! I'm SO lucky.' Tim, busy dad of four

She's a keeper, Tim.

THREE CHEERS for all the hands-on mums who willingly give up their own free time to help dad out with the school admin, kids' parties, homework and holiday planning.

Even if they don't always get it right, how wonderful that some mums aren't afraid to get stuck in. After all, is there anything sexier than a woman pushing a pram?

So-called solutions to inequality in the home

Fortunately, friends, family and media offer up a treasure trove of ideas for women struggling to balance work, parenting and housework, all of them comically ineffective and adding to mum's spiralling to-do list. For example:

Buy wellness products

Appealing to the individual, the wellness industry sells products to women promising to deliver more energy, balance and calm. This is how the same advice sounds when exaggerated and applied to men:

'I struggled to combine raising children with a high-powered job. Eating just 6 almonds a day gave me energy to tackle both.' Mark, age forty-five

'I manage to look great at the same time as running a successful business by using a gentle testicle mist.' David, age fifty-two, Dadpreneur

Working husband? How do you keep your energy levels up? 'I keep a radish in my wallet.' Ishan, age forty-seven

How do you balance work and fatherhood? 'I skip through fields, eat fresh fruits and veggies and stay hydrated.' Giovanni, age thirty-five

STRESS-STRICKEN DAD? Did you know that coconut oil has many benefits? It releases the hormone that tackles structural inequalities.

More than a little patronising, these posts highlight some of the absurd claims made by wellness products marketed at women. Also note that the change necessary here to achieve wellbeing is in women's hands and can be corrected with a simple purchase and mindset shift. If you embrace holistic health and look after your mind and body, this is apparently enough to achieve work/life balance. No big societal changes to address the root causes of women's burnout and stress are required. If the imbalance is within your own body, for example in your gut bacteria or vaginal pH, then the solution lies with the individual: drink a probiotic and moisturise your vulva. Problem sleeping because you have a six-month-old baby and a husband who won't do night feeds? Enjoy a peaceful night by getting an hour of sunlight exposure in the morning and spraying your pillow with a chamomile and snail mucin pillow spray. Job done.

Get up earlier

Another commonly trotted-out solution to the problem of women doing everything is to simply get up earlier.

WAKEY WAKEY, BUSY DADS! Now is a good time to do some gentle stretches, bake 25 mini quiches, make a stunning tulip arrangement and SMILE.

How do you stay organised in the summer hols? 'I get up 3 hours before my wife and kids to fit everything in.' Lee, forty-two

WAKEY WAKEY, BUSY DADS! Now is a good time to do the laundry because you won't have time over Easter. Smart dads get ahead. If you're really struggling, why not ask your wife to help?

Indeed, getting up early is something many mothers do because it is the only way to fit everything in. If you are doing all the jobs on the imaginary Liam's list, when do you have time to exercise, read or listen in peace to a podcast about time management or anxiety? The answer is never, unless you carve out time by sleeping less, which (see wellness advice above) you shouldn't be doing. It is a lose-lose solution for women. Sleep less to fit everything in, and you're not looking after yourself. Sleep well, and fail to get everything done.

Delegate chores

'My wife is great. She'll even take the kids to the doctors and dentists for me as I long as I book the appointments and remind her where to go and when. I'm SO lucky.' Paul, busy dad of three

'My wife will take the baby out on her own for an hour, as long as I pack the nappy bag, tell her exactly what to do and stay on the other end of the phone should she need me. I'm SO lucky.' Omar, career man and dad of one

Alongside getting up earlier, delegating chores to your husband is suggested by well-meaning friends, relatives and women's media as a solution to the mental and physical load. Many also advise that women should give men tasks they enjoy and encourage kids to help out by making tasks fun. Kindly as this advice may seem, delegating jobs and making chores into a game for kids becomes another task on her mushrooming list. 'Why not get your kids to pair socks?' is the advice cheerfully and innocently dished out by grandmas to mums who can't keep up with the laundry: grandmas who have forgotten that when you have a million other things to do, it's just easier to do it yourself.

Meanwhile, dad waits to be given jobs, even complaining he has been 'sent' to the shops or is 'babysitting' his own kids. He doesn't need to think about the task until she asks him to do it. It is still her job to notice or remember something needs doing. She then has the additional job of delegation and project management.

Go part-time

Returning to busy dad of three, Liam, if he's struggling, posters on Facebook ask whether he has thought about going down to two days a week? Maybe it's unrealistic for him to have a career and be a husband and be a dad at the same time? Perhaps he is being a little selfish and greedy, wanting it all?

> *'We both loved our jobs and earned the same, so it made sense for me to go part time when the kids came along.' Stephen, age thirty-seven*

> *TODAY'S DEBATE: Is it realistic for a busy dad to work full-time?*

> *'Women and men are equal but different. For example, men prioritise lower paid part-time jobs so they can do more unpaid caring work and we should absolutely celebrate that.' Katie, MP*

In on the joke, a woman on Twitter replies with:

> *Oh, we celebrate it alright. When our men sweat the mundane, small stuff, we are free to pursue our well-paid, high-status jobs. After all, no woman wants to spend her days chasing after children and cleaning toilets!*

Another woman on Twitter fakes outrage at the use of the word 'unpaid':

> *Unpaid? You're joking, aren't you? The Mr is paid alright. He has everything he could possibly want, a grocery budget that he can spend how he likes, fancy cleaning products, the best pet food money can buy, a new pair of trousers every month and a very expensive washing machine. He has everything a man could wish for, and more!*

Ask for help

Presented as a straightforward solution, women are often advised to simply ask for help if they are 'struggling'. Perhaps her husband or mum could babysit for a couple of hours? When you put the shoe on the other foot, the absurdity is revealed:

> *WAKEY WAKEY, BUSY DADS! Why not ask your wife to babysit today so you can get on with the housework? Relax and enjoy. Daddy heaven.*

> *TODAY'S DEBATE: Men are happier when they hire a cleaning gentleman to help them with their housework. But is it ethical?*

> *BUSY DAD? Saturday is YOUR day. Why not ask your wife to babysit for an hour so you can clean behind the fridge in peace? The worst she can say is no.*

When we imagine dad is entirely responsible for childcare and housework, we see the burden placed on women more clearly. The word 'help' is a massive clue. If two people are equally responsible for looking after their own child and home, one doesn't *help* the other. Instead, two people should be working together to get the jobs done.

Lower your standards

If none of the above strategies work, women are often encouraged to lower their standards. The assumption is always that a woman's standards are too high and need lowering, rather than that her husband's standards are too low and should be raised. Again, the onus is on the woman to adapt and change because she is responsible not only for doing everything, but also for learning how to live with this injustice by adjusting what she is willing to tolerate.

When exaggerated and switched, this advice is exposed as wrong-headed:

PRO TIP: If you struggle to get your wife to do her fair share of the childcare, it could be that your standards are too high, you use the wrong tone of voice or you criticise too much.

'My husband is always moaning about how much he has to do. He's so uptight and I'm sorry to have to say this, but no one wants a nagging husband.' Maryam

As this shows, complaining about having to do everything is also a no-no. Not only does Maryam's husband look unattractive when he complains, it's irritating. He should relax into his inequality instead of nagging and moaning. He doesn't want his wife to leave him for a younger man, does he?

Get therapy

Back in the real world, women are often encouraged to get, or resort to getting, therapy for problems associated with feeling overwhelmed like stress, anxiety and depression. One more time-consuming task for the list, and some therapists might encourage a woman to think that it is her family background or her personality that causes her to do too much in the home. Perhaps her attachment style or ADHD is to blame? Is she stressed because she's neglecting self-care? Has she forgotten how to breathe? Or maybe she is a natural rescuer and needs to look after other people to meet her own needs? Regardless of the diagnosis or label, the inference is that there is something wrong with her. In her book *Sexy But Psycho*, Dr Jessica Taylor talks about how psychiatry as a profession pathologises and medicates women for not conforming to social stereotypes. In her words, 'Psychiatry is the patriarchy with a prescription pad.' While Dr Taylor's work focuses on women who report abuse and are labelled psycho as a result, the same principle can be applied to women facing stress and burnout. Rather than seeing a woman's anxiety or anger as being a natural and rational response to bearing the brunt of the mental, emotional and physical load, the self-help and therapy industry often seeks to locate the problem within the woman – either her brain is lacking chemicals, or her hormones are playing up.

I am suspicious of any theoretical approach used by therapists that doesn't take into account power and inequality. It would seem a coincidence that most women are, for example, in transactional analysis terms, rescuers ('it's easier to do it myself') or persecutors ('nagging') in the home, with men tending towards victim status ('henpecked'). Might something else be going on here? Similarly, too many women 'happen' to have a personality type that makes them great organisers, shoppers and cleaners, leaving men free to benefit from these suspiciously unequally distributed traits.

Meanwhile, men are celebrated

Adding insult to injury is the fact that the men who do 'help' with childcare or housework are celebrated as heroes, as if they have bravely conquered their natural inability to fold clothes or plait hair. And if they do it without being asked and *willingly*, the apparent gold standard of a man's involvement in domestic duties, then even better. Imagine if we praised 'active, hands-on mums' for looking after their own children and ironing their *own* tops in the same way:

> THREE CHEERS for the women who willingly give up their own free time to help their husbands with the kids over Easter.

> 'I put my clean clothes away without being asked today!' Claire, CEO

Bravo Claire! Well done. We need more amazing women like you.

Taking this further, imagine a group of husbands in the pub chatting about their wives. One says, 'I'm so lucky. My wife is great – she takes the kids to the park for me on a Saturday.' The other replies, 'Mine is pretty good too – she doesn't mind babysitting for me when I go out.'

Why is this scenario so unlikely? It's because dads don't need to talk about any of this stuff; it is a non-issue. The home and family apparently run themselves, leaving them free to talk about work, sport and the news. At most, men might grumble about being nagged, but it would be rare to find a group of dads discussing stain removal or getting excited about a heated clothes dryer over a beer.

The feminist load

Rarely mentioned in wellness marketing or by therapists is the fact that it might not be your fault that you do too much. It might well be a structural issue caused by a variety of factors largely beyond your control. You probably *don't* have an iron deficiency. Maybe you are just tired because you don't get enough sleep and your brain is overwhelmed by the mental and emotional load. Your response is entirely rational and predictable.

However, it is apparently still your responsibility to do something about these bigger, societal issues. Unfortunately, this adds more to your to-do list in the form of reading feminist books and articles, sharing memes, listening to podcasts, marching, donating to charity, signing petitions and otherwise directing your anger positively towards progress and change. I call this 'the feminist load'. There is a certain irony in trying to stay awake while reading books such as *Shattered: Modern Motherhood and the Illusion of Equality* by Rebecca Asher while your husband plays *Destiny* on the PlayStation. Or you might find yourself getting excited about Eve Rodsky's book *Fair Play* and its accompanying card game that aims to help women to share household tasks and transform their lives. At last, something practical that you can use with your husband to get him to take on his fair share. But unfortunately you didn't have time to finish the book and you forgot to buy the card game. So the book sits alongside other unread gems such as Philippa Perry's *The Book You Wish Your Parents Had Read (and*

Your Children Will be Glad That You Did). Or, in my case, *(and Your Children Will be Disappointed That You Didn't)*.

Then comes the added load of having to complain to our friends about the inequalities we face as a form of therapy, another regular and draining commitment, and energy we could be spending elsewhere. Many turn to the Mumsnet talk boards for support, listing everything they do and asking, 'Am I Being Unreasonable (AIBU)?' For example, a woman having chemotherapy for breast cancer asks the heartbreaking question, 'Am I being unreasonable to ask my husband to hang the washing out while I'm in recovery from chemo?' Even more depressing can be a minority of responses in the comments, with some women voting yes, you are being unreasonable and others asking, 'Can't you do the laundry on your good days?' or, 'Could you ask your mum to help out?'

Sort out the next generation while you're at it

Not only is it a woman's responsibility to improve her own situation, she is also held responsible for the next generation, for example, apparently she is the one who should be talking to her boys about porn, educating the kids about online safety, avoiding clothes emblazoned with sexist slogans and providing good male role models. Another pretty bloody big job for her list. Where is the pressure on dads to do something about porn, including stopping watching it themselves? Why is the responsibility on mothers to find and keep a good male role model for her sons? Surely it is up to more men to actually *be* good role models, then we wouldn't have to scrat around to find one. And how sad that it should be a matter of 'finding' one; like finding a pair of shoes you can walk in or finding a comfortable bra. We rarely hear the phrase 'good female role models', presumably because we, and yes I mean you too, are ubiquitous. Imagine the luxury of not modelling good behaviour to our children, knowing that you were allowed to be a bit lax because the other parent would always pick up the pieces. Sign me up!

So what can be done about this shitstorm?

In order for women to feel less overwhelmed and shed some mental load, someone has to take it off her. In order for her to have more spare time, someone has to have less. In order for her to shed some responsibility, someone has to take some of it away. In order for her to enjoy more wellness, someone has to have less wellness. You might think kindly that there is enough wellness to go around. Plenty of free time for everyone. Nope, not when you have children. Things Need Doing and someone has to do them.

That someone is the husband, dad or partner. Him doing more and her doing less is the solution. Imagine if instead of telling women that they are responsible for doing too much, we told men that they are responsible for doing too little. Imagine books, TV shows and memes talking about the phenomenon of The Man Who Does Too Little, replacing the Woman Who Does Too Much trope. Imagine how conversations would change in families, in parenting articles and men's magazines.

No more triathlons

Imagine if men were actively discouraged from prioritising their own wellness and instead were told they need to look after themselves *only* to look after others. This would mean no more training for triathlons, mammoth bike rides, time-consuming hobbies, hours in the shed or gaming. The message would be to lay down your feelgood hobbies and dopamine-rich competitive sport. Give up your 'man-cave' because you won't need that as an active and equal member of an adult couple. You need only keep yourself fit and well enough for housework and running after kids. Shaving seconds off your personal best is not necessary for folding fitted sheets. You can bend down and empty the washing machine without going to CrossFit.

No, *you* get up earlier

Does that sound a bit unfair and you still want to go fell running? You're not ready to give up golf? Well maybe you should have thought of that before you had kids. Imagine if the message for dads was that the *only* way to fit in a weekday gym session or weekend run was to get up earlier. How does 4 a.m. sound? It's amazing what you can do before your wife and kids get up. Just don't forget to breathe!

No, *you* go part time

Imagine if we not only encouraged but *expected* dads to go part time after they have children. If it wasn't for the gender pay gap plaguing so many couples, this would make as much sense as it does currently for mum to go part time. And the skills you learn as a househusband can be useful in the workplace!

No, *you* raise *your* standards

Imagine if men all suddenly got off the sofa and started to clean, taking feedback from their wives on their efforts and acting on it. And imagine if men did this without announcing what they have just done afterwards, just getting on with it silently and doing it properly. Because as an adult, keeping your house clean and tidy is actually normal and age-appropriate. No praise necessary.

No, *you* get therapy

If you can't hack this advice and you think it's not fair, that would of course be your problem because other dads do it, so why can't you? So maybe you need to see a therapist. A good therapist will help you to iron out any personality disorder, hormonal problems or attachment issues that might be preventing you from cleaning, organising and batch cooking. If giving up darts to look after your own children makes you miserable, perhaps your penis pH is unbalanced, or maybe you have a vitamin deficiency?

No, *you* read all the books

First read all the books your wife has suggested over the years, all the ones about parenting and feminism, including *Fair Play* and French cartoonist Emma's books *Mental Load* and *Emotional Load*. This will free her up to go for a run, catch up with some work or lie on the sofa with her phone in peace. Go back through your emails and messages and read all the articles she suggested but you didn't bother to read. Then do your own research, learn about housework,

Flipping Patriarchy

parenting and relationships. Don't tell her all about it or ask her what she thinks, just read, learn and then do the stuff.

Reject hero status

Done all this and more? You're still not a hero or a super-dad. You're just doing the normal things required to be in an adult relationship, living in a sanitary house with happy and healthy children. Whoop-de-fucking-do.

Ending on a low

Back to Mum, the actual hero in all of this; the true legend who deserves a break for the next few centuries. If after years of trying different strategies to get him to take responsibility – the shared calendar on your phone, the spreadsheet of tasks, the weekly planner on the fridge – you're *still* asking yourself, 'For fuck's sake, why do I have to do everything?' on a daily basis, you could always try Linda's strategy in *The Change*, Bridget Christie's menopause comedy. Linda, the tired mum of two teenagers, played by Christie, logs the amount of time she spends doing household tasks; for example, washing up: eleven minutes; tidying away after her own fiftieth birthday party: twenty-five minutes. Each chore is timed and logged in a ledger, stored in the kitchen drawer. We find out that Linda has been keeping these ledgers for many years, when her husband, Steve, accidently finds dozens of them tumbling out of a top cupboard. The punchline is watching him read the entry 'sex with Steve' amongst all the cleaning, organising and tidying tasks, and then finding out this particular note in the ledger took no more than two minutes of Linda's time. But away from TV, in your own invisible life, watched by no one, who would you show your ledgers to? And would they even care?

If your domestic situation has gone well beyond comedy, you could always turn to the Mumsnet talk boards for support from veterans on these matters. You would not be the first woman to ask on the 'Am I Being Unreasonable?' talk board for advice on the division of labour between you and your husband. However, be warned. On the question of a husband or partner who doesn't pull his weight, and especially when presented with an unequal list of responsibilities, seasoned mums on the talk boards are quick to dispatch three letters of advice, often with no explanation. LTB stands for Leave The Bastard. And, unlike @manwhohasitall's posts, these women are often deadly serious.

The Mental Load

- Researching everything
- Anticipating everything
- Deciding everything
- Remembering everything
- Noticing everything
- Knowing everything
- Project managing everything
- Doing something about the fact that you do everything
- And don't forget to smile!

3.

Not Just a Pretty Beard

The women on the TV makeover show *10 Years Younger in 10 Days* look exhausted and careworn. Many of them have spent a lifetime looking after others, their days consumed with raising children and other care work. Some are recovering from serious illnesses or trauma. We watch as people chosen at random on the street guess the age of these hard-working, responsible women and pass judgement on their appearance: 'could make more of an effort', 'let herself go', 'looks tired'.

In the middle part of the show, we watch as she learns from the experts how to disguise the dark circles under her eyes using three little dots of concealer, apply eyeshadow to make her eyes pop and wear clothes that flatter her big tummy. More dramatic transformations are achieved with new teeth veneers, Botox, fillers, hair extensions, peels and laser treatments. The emphasis is on concealing, erasing and covering up what society considers unacceptable, and highlighting, revealing or adding what is associated with youth and beauty.

After ten days of cosmetic treatments, dentistry, a new wardrobe and a makeover, it's back to the street to ask the

Flipping Patriarchy

public to guess the contestant's age for a second time. Success is declared when the public believe the woman is her real age, or, ideally, ten years younger. Friends and family can't believe the change, declaring that 'she's got her sparkle back'. A supportive husband is often overwhelmed by the sight of his revamped wife: 'I kept telling her to do something for herself, and she's finally done it.'

The narrative throughout the programme is that looking good helps you to feel good, improve your confidence and find yourself. We are reminded by the presenter, as the top layer of the contestant's skin is peeled off, that the show is all about how you feel on the inside, and you can tell that she believes it. The women say they are doing it for themselves. But as I watch *10 Years Younger in 10 Days*, and other similar programmes, I can't help feeling the efforts of the experts, while clearly appreciated by the contestants at the time, are misplaced. Maybe what the woman really needs, instead of a more flattering haircut and a cropped leather jacket, is affordable childcare, a pay increase and some respect and appreciation from those around her. Instead of issuing instructions to his wife to relax from his chair, the husband could get out of his chair and share the load. As unrealistic, worthy and intrusive as this format idea may sound, it is actually a no more ridiculous proposition than the real show.

In my version of the programme, responsibility for the transformation would lie as much with other people as with the contestant; for example, with her family, friends and workplace. The current show puts all the emphasis on the role of the individual to improve her own body image and pays no attention to identifying and eliminating the cause of her insecurities. In my new anti-fun show, experts would make efforts to improve the material circumstances that contribute to her tiredness and lack of self-esteem. Does she receive equal pay? Is she one of the hundreds of thousands of people entitled to benefits but not claiming them? Does she need support in advocating for her kids?

To improve her mental wellbeing in the short term, experts would help her do more of the things we know boost wellbeing such as being active, learning a new skill and connecting with others. If she's too busy for any of this, the presenter could enlist the help of friends and family to ease her burden and free up time so she can look after herself. This wouldn't make for a grand unveiling at the end, where the contestant's glamorous new look is revealed in a mirror, but has more hope of a lasting change, and would have absolutely nothing to do with her appearance, thus not reinforcing the idea that a woman's worth is contingent on looking young and attractive.

Rather than asking people to guess the contestant's age at the start of the show, they could be quizzed on what they think her occupation is. Regardless of the answers, members of the public would be told exactly what she does. For example, 'she's a single mum bringing up three kids, all with additional needs, and is recovering from a serious accident.' Then would come a description of what she does on a day-to-day basis. A selection of reactions from passers-by would be chosen and played back to the contestant and viewers. Rather than comments like 'she looks frumpy', we would expect to

Flipping Patriarchy

hear validating feedback such as 'wow', 'she's amazing' and 'I can't believe anyone can do so much in a day.' Instead of being judged on her appearance, she would be admired for her hard work, resilience and determination; what she does and who she is, not what she looks like. The fact that her life shows on her face would be irrelevant, and the message that a woman's worth correlates with her appearance would not be reinforced in her head or anyone else's.

If, by the end of the ten days, she said, 'I came on this show for free Botox and lip fillers, not to be lectured,' the presenter could interview feminists, psychologists, academics and other experts on the powerful cultural forces, messages and beliefs that cause women to want to look younger. This would give the viewer context about why women choose to have these treatments. It is not because we are silly, vain or shallow. It's because we are brainwashed from a young age that being pretty and youthful is our ticket to self-worth, success and social acceptance. This is reinforced by the media's obsession with the age and appearance of celebrities (mostly women) and viral beauty products that promise to turn back the clock.

The contestant could then decide, off-camera, whether to have the treatments, with zero judgement from the presenter or anyone else. The viewers wouldn't find out whether she goes ahead, because we don't care. By now we are rooting for her. We just want her to feel better, in order to feel better, full stop.

After the show, she would have less to do, not more. She may not feel compelled to add regular Botox, hair extensions and a daily skincare regime to her to-do list, even after a well-deserved 10 per cent pay rise. The shadows under her eyes would still be there, but she would hardly notice, realising that life is too precious to spend it pretending to look not-tired and not-cross when you actually are, and for good reason. With her burden eased and with more time to spend doing things that are shown to improve mental health, her confidence may indeed return. She might even be less knackered and less cross on the inside, which would be a genuine win. If she 'gets her sparkle back', this will not be down to fake tan, a cheek tint and an illuminating primer claiming to 'light up skin from within'. It will be because she is getting more sleep and has more time to herself. Instead of looking ten years younger, she would be ten years lighter, with the weight of responsibility and the pressure of looking good lifted. The name of the show, *10 Years Younger in 10 Days*, would change to *10 Fewer Fucks to Give* because by the end of the show, she would give ten fewer fucks about how she looks. I suspect this updated version of the show would be popular, with many applications to take part.

While we have the dad out of his chair and on his feet, let's imagine he is under the same pressure as his wife is to look good. His name is Liam, the same Liam from Chapter 2 who was complaining about his never-ending to-do list. Liam is thirty-nine, married with three kids and is beginning to show signs of ageing: fine lines, forehead wrinkles, dull skin, a dry beard, marionette lines and grey hairs. Like most dads his age, Liam checks Facebook and Instagram throughout the day and gets email newsletters from his favourite shops. He also gets Google alerts on his phone and finds himself reading them mindlessly in quiet moments.

Let's imagine a typical day for Liam in September. The kids are back at school and the nights are drawing in. Liam wakes up at 6 a.m. and the first thing he does before anything else is think about how he should be drinking a glass of warm water with lemon juice to rejuvenate his skin. While drinking his coffee, he reads the latest recommended articles from Google:

- Men in their seventies love this hair mousse that Michael Douglas is using
- Shop the ten best oils for dry beards
- Martin Freeman, fifty-three, reveals the secret to his healthy glowing skin
- The firming testicle cream so good it sells every eight seconds
- 'Ken' Botox and other ways to keep your neck youthful and smooth

He orders the firming testicle cream from Amazon after reading the latest reviews and remembering how bouncy and tight they used to look. He hopes it arrives the next day so he can use it for two weeks, the average time it takes to see visible results and just in time for his birthday weekend away. The article about beard oil makes him feel guilty; he has two similar products already, a luxe beard serum and a budget beard primer, but doesn't use either of them. He puts a reminder on his phone to find the serum and start using it: LIAM! BEARD OIL!

While doing his morning face yoga, he thinks about the

ridiculous pressure on men to look young while he scrutinises his neck in the mirror and concludes that it looks all wrong. Is it too short? Or is his head too narrow? Maybe he should get Ken Botox? Would anyone notice? Might it cause bruising? Would it look odd? He gets back into bed and googles before-and-after pictures. Ten minutes later and it's time to pick up towels, clear the breakfast things away and make sure the kids are nearly ready for school. He dresses the little one, finds and fills up the water bottles and leaves everything next to the front door for his wife. While the kids get dressed, he starts his pared-down skincare regime: a Vitamin C cleansing wash, his new age-denial peptastic serum, sea cucumber eyebrow mist, retinol water day cream (SPF 90) and a mushroom face setting spray. He checks out the luminosity of his face in three different mirrors in the house and says to himself mockingly, 'Ready, steady, glow!' With his skin prepped, he races downstairs to remind his wife to take three water bottles, three bags, three coats and three children to school on her way to work. A quick scan of the hall and he can see that she's forgotten two water bottles, one bag, two coats and one child. He flings open the door and catches her just in time.

It's his 'day off', as his wife calls it: keeping on top of work emails, laundry, baking, tidying, hoovering, cleaning, batch cooking and school admin. While his second load of washing is in and his healthy blackberry muffins are baking, he checks his inbox:

- £15 off Be Handsome Advent Calendar
- John Torode reveals why he tried a salmon roe facial

Flipping Patriarchy

- Get that new-trousers feeling
- DIY Bald Head Scrub: Top ten ways to groom your scalp at home
- Barber explains why we get frizzy chest hair and how to stop it for good

Liam thinks back to last year's Be Handsome advent calendar and wonders whether it was worth it. He didn't tell anyone about the purchase in case they thought he was wasting money. He opened the individual boxes secretly in twenty-four tiny acts of self-hate. Inside he discovered a caffeine serum to reduce under-eye puffiness, a volumizing shampoo to lift his limp, lifeless hair, a mist to purify his blackhead-clogged face and a full-size bottle of illuminating forearm primer. The eye serum made no visible difference, his youngest tipped the shampoo into the bath before he could even try it, he couldn't tell if his face was more or less pure after fourteen days of misting and the illuminating forearm primer was sticky, attracting cat hairs instead of compliments. It was worth it for the retinol triple booster, he thinks, as he excitedly signs up for exclusive early access to this year's ultimate calendar, complete with fourteen full-size products!

As Liam hangs out the washing, his mind turns to coats. This year, he thinks, he will find the perfect coat: simple, stylish and practical. This coat will solve autumn and winter. Indeed, it will solve more than that: it will solve Liam himself. It will be ideal for any occasion so he will only need one. Just one coat. He imagines himself throwing it on casually with any outfit. The perfect coat will go with any trouser length; it will be warm, waterproof, smart, classic, iconic, effortless, quality, timeless, chic and practical. Finding it will be a lifelong ambition ticked off, a satisfaction like no other. It will be a true mark of adulthood, a coat that he can wear without overthinking, or indeed without any thinking. It will be the most normal and natural thing in the world. Liam will become one hundred percent coat. He concludes, without exaggeration, that finding the perfect coat will complete him.

Energised by the thought of something so big ticked off his to-do list, Liam gets through his jobs: top up school dinner balance, reply to a party invite, check work emails, return consent form for flu jab, online food shop, sign middle one up for school choir, email football club, drink three litres of water, google how to get rid of fruit flies and text his wife to remind her to pick up the kids early for their dentist appointment. With just an hour left until they get home, Liam remembers he has three parcels to return to the post office: a shirt in a colour that drains him, a pair of jeans that flatten his bum and a navy duffle coat that, rather than signalling adulthood, makes him look like a toddler. Sometimes it's hard to be a man, he thinks.

Twenty minutes later, after finally deciding which of his four (most easily accessible) coats to wear, Liam leaves the house, returning three minutes later because he's too hot. He thinks this is what they mean about transitional coats, then wonders where on earth you are supposed to store them all. The idea of transitional clothing leads to fantasies about the ultimate capsule wardrobe, investment pieces, clever layering and outfits that take you from day to night. On the way back to the post office, Liam feels like a failure; he can't even leave the house successfully, let alone master effortless autumn styling. At least he's getting his steps in though; all good progress towards living an active lifestyle, or losing weight as he used to call it.

In his final few minutes before the kids pile in, Liam checks his inbox:

- Are you a coat person?
- New season coats
- You've been washing your moustache all wrong
- Coat cravings
- Lean into layers

The front door opens; bags and coats are flung to the ground. An instrument skids down the hall and crashes into a door. Liam hears the fridge open, footsteps and then silence; the sounds of snacks and screens. Claire shouts to Liam to ask him what's for dinner and then disappears into her office without waiting for an answer. After putting three ultra-processed pizzas in the oven, Liam thinks about what to wear to go out later in the week. Different versions of himself come to mind, but he doesn't have the shoes to go with all of them, so he settles for 'no effort' Liam. This involves a grey hoodie that doesn't cling to his hips and fits under his leather jacket. He pairs the hoodie with jeans, specially designed for the angular male body that skim his crotch, cradle his bottom and flatter his calves. He thinks

Not Just a Pretty Beard

about the best time to wash his hair (the day before) and wonders how he's going to fit everything in.

After he's made dinner, emptied and refilled the dishwasher, tidied the hall, and got the breakfast things ready, Liam finds himself sitting on the stairs picking bits off the carpet. He pauses to check his phone:

- Shoppers love 'slimming trousers' that are perfect for autumn
- All grown up! James Acaster flaunts his gorgeous curls in new show
- The four best ways to take collagen, according to a dietician
- Ten quick stubble fixes to bring life to autumn beards
- Common 52p store-cupboard ingredient to help your penis grow

It's late, and Liam still hasn't taken his collagen supplement; no wonder he looks so washed out. He goes downstairs to make a smoothie to dissolve the powder in, carrying a basket of dirty washing on the way, but gets distracted as he realises the kids are all still up. It's his wife's turn to get them to bed but she's fast asleep on the sofa, empty glass of wine on the coffee table, mouth open, phone in hand. *For fuck's sake*, he thinks, *nothing gets done around here unless I do it.* On his way to tell the little one he has five more minutes on his tablet watching inappropriate videos on YouTube, something big and damp, probably food, sticks to his slippers, reminding him about the fruit flies. As he scrapes the crushed pineapple off his soles and dries them with the last piece of kitchen roll, he thinks of one consolation in all this: at least raw fruit counts as a whole food; it's not ultra-processed like everything else the kids eat. And surely fresh pineapple is worth more because it is bright yellow and has a giant spiky stalk. If something so natural can't offset preservatives and emulsifiers, nothing can. Finally something for his gratitude journal, if he remembers to complete it.

Meanwhile, Liam's sixteen-year-old son, Oscar, is on his sixth hour of tutorials on how to achieve Korean glass skin and the reflective cheekbones of his dreams. To achieve an ultra-luminous complexion, he needs to flood his skin with moisture from the minute he wakes up. His mum says he already looks gorgeous and should stop obsessing about his appearance. Oscar could be revising for his A levels and playing sport like his cousin, Eva. Instead, he is saving to get the popular cosmetic filler treatment known as 'cunnilingus lips' when he turns eighteen. Two of his friends have had it done and he thinks they look great, now the swelling has gone down. Oscar's mum, Claire, does not approve and Liam despairs. He thinks things are even worse now than they were for him, especially after seeing tips on TikTok for boys on how they can look good in bed, from various angles and while performing certain sex acts.

With the kids finally in bed, Liam returns to the kitchen in his socks and resolves to tackle the flies. Google tells him to fill a pint glass with cider vinegar, washing-up liquid and water and then place a layer of cling film over the top. He makes three fly traps, forgetting to add the cling film, and places one on the wooden coffee table with a saucer underneath it to protect the varnish. It's getting late now, but not too late for a bath. *Time just for me*, he thinks, as he walks into the bathroom, imagining a spa-like sanctuary. The grotty reality hits him as he gathers up seven towels, pulls the plug, empties the cold water and picks out the toys, still covered in bubbles and something black, probably mould. One more thing for his to-do list: wash bath toys. As he fills the tub with fresh water, he mops the soaking floor with the bath mat and cleans the sink with his wife's flannel, carefully putting it back where he found it. *That'll teach her to leave everything for me to do*, he thinks, in a moment of spite. He wonders how long it would take before his wife noticed the bath mat needed replacing with a clean one. Until it decayed, he concludes, realising, not for the first time, that having a wife is like having another child.

While Liam obediently exfoliates his body for the third time that week, he contemplates the products lined up along the side of the bath. His body wash contains shea butter and coconut oil. It promises softer, silkier, smoother skin after just one use, and is part of a bath ritual range featuring eleven other must-have products (use together for maximum benefit). Claire's shower gel is called 'Woman Wash'; there's no mention of ingredients or benefits. The other bottles tell a similar story. Liam researched his shampoo carefully after reading many reviews; it's for dry, damaged hair in need of deep nourishment and maximum shine. He has tried many shampoos but keeps coming back to this one. If he uses a different product, his hair is a disaster and the day is ruined. Claire's shampoo bottle, by contrast, only has the words 'Shampoo for Women' printed on the front, more of a prescription than a marketing message. Liam imagines a different life, one where he doesn't have to worry about the texture of his hair or the softness of his skin. *Just imagine how much time I would have*, he thinks, picturing himself enjoying a glass of wine after a long day without a care in the world, followed by a snooze on the sofa.

On his way downstairs to take his collagen supplement he finds his wife in the kitchen rinsing out a pint glass in the sink. The room smells like the toilets at a cider festival: sweet, foamy and apple-y, with a hint of artificial lemon. Claire says, 'What did you put in that drink you left out for me? I couldn't finish it.' Liam does a tiny smile; he knows exactly what happened. Claire must have woken up with a dry mouth after drinking the wine, looked directly in front of her and saw what she assumed was a pint of homemade lemonade nicely presented on a saucer. *That must be for me*, she thought, *I'll drink it*. Unmoved by the thought of his wife drinking vinegar, washing-up liquid and flies, Liam thinks to himself, *Oh dear,* and reaches for his collagen supplement. Tomorrow morning, he resolves, he will replace the fly trap his wife drank and find the source of the infestation.

It's a month later and Liam is googling 'Men's Halloween costumes': sexy wizard, sexy bat, sexy skeleton, sexy ghost, sexy moth. Claire is apparently going as herself; a joke Liam has heard a hundred times before. She just can't be arsed to make an effort and doesn't have to. Like all the other women, she will wear a top and jeans and may or may not ask Liam to put eyeliner on her in the last ten minutes before they leave the house. He orders sexy skeleton bodycon trousers and a sexy batwing shirt . The expression 'seasonally sexy' occurs to him as he goes through the checkout. Not only is Liam expected to be decorative and just-the-right-kind of sexy all year round, but he must also change his appearance to reflect the season. There is summer sexy ('Beach Body Ready'), Halloween sexy (vamp), winter sexy (cosy), Christmas sexy (glam) and even Easter sexy (cute bunny). Fortunately, Liam has the legs for Halloween, making sexy skeleton the obvious choice. He worries he might be Too Much in his costume, a thought he has regularly about his body. And not just Too Much for Halloween, but Too Much overall. He used to ask his wife if his bum looked too big, then his attention turned to his knees; are they too low down, or is his top half too long? Lately he has worried more about his overall presence – is he simply too big from the front? Or too big from the side? Too big close-up? Claire just laughs and tells him he looks lovely, even when he doesn't make an effort. Unfortunately, Claire has no idea how much time goes into looking like you haven't made an effort.

Three weeks until the Christmas party and Liam still hasn't perfected a professional brow or finalised his show-stopping outfit. He is now worried about being Not Enough. His head is swimming with sparkly trousers, glitzy wallets, joyful decorations and exquisitely wrapped presents. This year, he will be happy, handsome, calm and organised. Or at least he will be when his festive cold sore heals and he loses enough weight to be able to put it all back on over Christmas. Once he gets his normal, unblistered mouth back and the bloating subsides, he

Flipping Patriarchy

will be able to enjoy life again, and be a proper person. Until then, he resolves, he will focus on sorting his festive fashion. Liam turns to the Christmas edition of *Man and Home*, the glossy men's magazine his dad bought him a subscription for last year. He casts an eye over the front cover:

- Sleigh, boy, sleigh!
- Winter crafting dads
- Dazzling trousers
- Christmas wrapping with Ashley Cole
- 603 ways to look 100 per cent hot!
- Unwrap total biceps confidence: your gift to you!
- David Attenborough: How he found his inner WOW

Still searching for his outer wow, Liam orders a pair of glam trousers and a Christmas sweater, hoping these two purchases will see him through Christmas. He wants to make an impression without being over the top; not an easy line to tread. Soon after the email receipts land in his inbox, he remembers the five party shirts and seven Christmas jumpers he already owns but couldn't find if he tried amongst the bags of children's clothes, sentimental linens, paperwork and summer trousers. Christmas, he thinks, is just another opportunity to feel like a failure, a festive failure: non-exquisite wrapping, inedible gifts, boring hair and centrally heated skin. In the end, the simple and stylish, stress-free Christmas Liam dreams of turns into an exhausting shitshow. Meanwhile, Claire says how much she loves Christmas: the opportunity to relax and do nothing.

It's New Year and Liam has tidied Christmas away. All his

dad friends say it's nice to 'get back to normal' while the women complain about having to go back to work after such a lovely break. As Claire boasts that she doesn't believe in New Year's resolutions at the same time as patting her expanding waistline, Liam is now in self-improvement mode. This year will be your year to shine, his phone tells him. All he has to do is master six super-powered soups, teach himself to be happy and let go of guilt. But first he must find the source of the urine smell upstairs. The house smells like a farm, he thinks, as he sniffs the carpet, beds and bins in every room. If he could just make the inside of his house cleaner than the outside, he would be happy. Is that too much to ask?

Two birthday parties and a school trip later and Valentine's Day is looming. Liam must perform a special role: a sexy, smiling, doe-eyed siren. Will this year be his most handsome Valentine's Day yet? Liam again turns to his *Man and Home* magazine for advice on how to achieve the perfect sultry eye on the most romantic day of the year. Unfortunately, Liam is feeling less sexy than ever, hopefully something he can remedy with a few simple tricks. He wonders if he should opt for doe-eyes this year. Apparently larger, rounder and wider than the cat eye, Liam orders four new cult products to achieve the look, including one described as 'fourteen hours' sleep in a jar'. If only, he thinks, after weeks of disrupted nights caused by poorly children and noisy building work next door. He opens his eyes as wide as they will go and takes a selfie. Concluding he looks more weird than ever, Liam closes the magazine and turns his attention to reading about diet secrets of the stars on his phone. Ever wonder what Prince

William eats in a day? Not once, he says to himself, as he reads on, making a mental note to eat smaller portion sizes and pay more attention to the colour of his food.

Liam doesn't enjoy Valentine's Day. His wife gives him a thoughtless card and box of chocolates, exactly what he doesn't want after bingeing over Christmas. The portion sizes in the restaurant are enormous and all the food is beige with not one colour of the rainbow represented. Claire asks Liam why he has a sweaty face in the taxi on the way there; his dreams of a luminous, youthful glow are shattered. All those hours planning his dreamy, romantic look for nothing. The evening's ruination is complete when Claire asks Liam if he is okay for the fifth time. Far from looking relaxed, happy and gorgeous, Liam fears he looks exactly how he feels: tense, angry and disappointed. Certainly the natural look, but not the one he intended. The least Claire could do is not make it worse. If only, like his wife, Liam could pull on the first half-decent top he clapped eyes on. Beyond having a clean face, preferably without crumbs or ketchup around the corners of her mouth, Claire is required to make zero effort. *Happy fucking Valentine's Day*, he says to himself as he goes to sleep, high on salted caramels, cheesecake and crisps. The least romantic day of the year.

Fast forward to spring and Liam has reached what he thought would be his 'happy weight'. Except it isn't as happy as he thought. He is plagued by thoughts that he looked better with a bit of weight on him (something to hold on to) and is now 'too thin' with a gaunt face. His grandad used to say older men have to choose between their face or their body; Liam now knows what he meant and

Not Just a Pretty Beard

wonders whether choosing his body at the expense of his face is the right decision. He imagines friends and family whispering about him, asking Claire if he's eating enough. No one says 'you look well' anymore, and Liam doesn't know if this is a good or a bad thing. He looks back at photos from four Christmases ago and homes in on a photo of himself smiling, drink in hand with a flushed face. How did he not realise how handsome he was back then? Undeterred, Liam concludes he simply must look better slimmer and can finally become what his brother-in-law calls a clothes horse. Everything Liam tries on suits him. Except the clothes that hang off him. And the ones that drown him. And the ones that hide his shape. *You can't win*, Liam thinks as he turns to Instagram for inspiration.

- Botox for your beard
- The strawberry boy aesthetic
- Eleven-hour moustache
- How to have a lazy-boy summer
- Achieve the perfect pineapple mullet
- Chris Packham, sixty-two, on the daily habit that is a must for glowing skin

How is he going to fit all this in when he has his home to declutter, his relationship to fix and his wardrobe to overhaul? And the bath toys are still a health hazard six months after he first noticed the mould. About this time of year, Liam decides he has an iron and/or vitamin B_{12} deficiency and orders a shitload of supplements, every positive review fuelling his fantasy recovery. He also commits to drinking a probiotic every day to restore the natural balance of his testicle bacteria. The new Liam will have limitless energy, dewy, wrinkle-free skin and a positive outlook. Wellness Liam will get up early, before his wife and kids, to make easy banana bread and prepare a simple, nutritious breakfast involving overnight oats and fresh blueberries. Probiotic Liam will hang out his laundry wearing a pristine white shirt with a gorgeous smile on his natural, freckled face. Perfect, future Liam is so blissfully happy his eyes are shut so he can take in the fresh, spring air. At last Liam is content, on top of the laundry, in control of household smells and at peace with his body.

But the vitamins arrive and actual Liam forgets to take them, seriously jeopardising his transformation. Every room smells like wet dogs. He imagines what the house would smell like if they actually had a dog. But he doesn't have time to think about damp pets or supplements right now, more important matters have overtaken him: Easter crafts, finding the perfect mac and sorting out childcare over the holidays. Life is relentless, Liam thinks as he turns to TikTok for comfort:

- Static moustache hack
- Nail the Tomato Boy aesthetic
- Snow mushroom chest hair serum
- The Latte Beard tutorial
- Marcus Brigstocke debuts new look in preppy knitted jumper and fitted trousers

After ordering the mushroom serum and wondering whether he can pull off the Tomato Boy aesthetic at thirty-nine, Liam searches for something to wear for his brother's wedding. He avoids anything navy; he doesn't want to upstage the groom. Unfortunately, navy is this season's colour, making it difficult – 'typical boy problems', his wife tells him lovingly. He finally settles on a mid-blue suit, with masculine detail on the shoulders. The trousers would be perfect if they had pockets, Liam thinks, although he remembers something he once read, that pockets ruin a man's silhouette, certainly not something he is prepared to risk. The wedding is glorious, his brother did a fantastic job organising it all and everyone agreed the groom looked gorgeous.

It's time to pack for the family holiday and Liam's stress levels are through the roof. His dreams of a lazy-boy summer are fading, as he remembers how he felt on the return from last year's holiday: like a survivor; his life, relationship and mental health changed irrevocably for the worse. His only relief was supportive comments from other dads on the Dadsnet talk board who were all suffering similar 'holidays', with everyone agreeing they would rather be at home, where at least they were surrounded by their own stuff and weren't under constant threat from fathers-in-law, extreme weather events and divorce. But this year Liam is 'Beach Body Ready', a fact that should sustain him through the long car journeys, intermittent Wi-Fi and inevitable queues for toilets. Last year he told himself he was doing it for the kids, as he watched them slumped on the sofa in the villa on their phones, demanding snacks and refusing to brush their teeth. Claire, on the other hand, loves holidays and even packed her own case this year, something Liam wrote in his gratitude journal, wondering afterwards that if Claire pulled her fucking weight, maybe he wouldn't need a gratitude journal. He wouldn't be scraping the barrel every day for anything he could find that wasn't a disappointment, burden or injustice. AND ANOTHER THING, he didn't shout or even say out loud: why do so few women write gratitude journals? Is it because they simply don't have to? They take it all for granted, and don't have to comb through the day desperately looking for things to be grateful for. This insight changes nothing, as Liam completes his journal and goes to sleep on his back to avoid wrinkles, dreaming about cosy knits and the perfect winter coat.

The Quadruple Shift

And that whole thing of course, was a dream, a fantasy and a nonsense. No one called Liam thinks like this. It is women who face the onslaught of advice about how to look decades younger, find the perfect cashmere jumper and get a natural, radiant glow. And at times, we are even mocked and humiliated for the effort we put into looking good.

In 'The Hotel Inspectors', an episode of the seventies TV sitcom *Fawlty Towers*, the woman-hating Basil Fawlty (watch it again if you don't believe me) says to his wife, Sybil Fawlty, 'Oh dear! What happened? Did you get entangled in the eiderdown again? Hmm? Not enough cream in your éclair? Or did you have to talk to all your friends for so long that you didn't have time to perm your ears?' There is exaggeration, mockery and contempt in the idea of a woman perming her ears. But is this really such a ridiculous proposition now, given that we perm our eyelashes and laminate our brows? The writers of *Fawlty Towers* today would have to find new jokes.

The concept of the triple shift – being a mother, managing the home and working – seems dated and incomplete now. Women now face the quadruple shift, with the beauty load taking up a considerable amount of time and head space. Looking good, or just looking acceptable, is a full-time occupation in itself, never mind paid work or motherhood. And while some women do live happily without this pressure, the vast majority perform some degree of beauty work. Many women believe it is fun and harmless, just part and parcel of being a woman; natural, even. Others insist they are doing it entirely for themselves; a lovely idea, but something of a coincidence that we are all trying to look younger and prettier in the same way for ourselves. Others might blame commercialism and say it's simply about marketing and what sells, with no further questions about why only women are buying it. The idea that we want to look good for other women is also trotted out unthinkingly, as if men don't notice any of it and would be more than happy if we all just wore sacks (without a belt around the middle to accentuate our waists). The narrative therefore is that the beauty load is our own fault, both as individuals and as a group, and if we don't like it, we can opt out, it's our choice. Problem solved.

But this is to misunderstand the bigger issue and what is at stake. The beauty load is seriously gendered. This is obvious when we ask Caitlin Moran's question 'Are the men doing

Flipping Patriarchy

it?' Are the teenage boys learning how to get a 'glow-up'? Are the men in their twenties considering getting preventative Botox and investing in prejuvenation? Are the men in their forties applying anti-wrinkle tape to their faces? Are the men in their fifties obsessed with skincare? Are the men in their sixties feeling bad about their necks? (see Nora Ephron's *I Feel Bad About My Neck, and Other Thoughts on Being a Woman*). Are the men in their seventies finally happy with their bodies? Does your husband have a jade roller? Does your boyfriend want chrombre nails? Does your grandad apply castor oil at night to lock in the moisture? The answer to all these questions is no. And two or three new ranges of men's grooming products on the high street plus a handful of famous male make-up influencers does not equal 'men are under the same pressure to look good too'. One unused beard oil and an unopened tub of hair clay on the bathroom shelf and I am not convinced.

Middle-aged mums and dads blame social media for the pressure on young women to spend so much time working on their appearance, attempting to look #flawless. In particular, they might point to the influence of Instagram and TikTok, ridiculing the relatively new trend for thick, dark eyebrows which are not to their taste, but not inherently better or worse than the nineties skinny brow (both require maintenance and products). Meanwhile, the same middle-aged mums are worrying about their own eyebrows (too sparse?), even with the advantage of age and experience. The middle-aged men apparently can't get their heads around it, claiming they like natural women and that they actually (big round of applause) prefer women without make-up. Although presumably some of these men also consume porn, given that the majority of middle-aged men (57 per cent aged between thirty and forty-nine) report having watched pornography in the last month; a higher proportion than in any other age group[1]. Are these same men watching porn featuring women with natural pubic hair, of average weight and wearing no make-up? No, they are not. Neither do they seem to realise, as many women joke, that achieving the natural look requires a whole battalion of products including carefully chosen skincare, applied in the right order.

But never mind what individual men think or like, this is an issue of the patriarchy, the system that reinforces male dominance and men's oppression of women. According to Naomi Wolf, author of the nineties classic *The Beauty Myth*, as women spend more time on their appearance, their focus on freedom and equal rights is de-prioritised. We simply don't have time to see what is happening. We are too busy practising our wedding make-up to notice our fiancé has done fuck all to contribute to the occasion, heralding a pattern that will last a lifetime, unless Mumsnet radicalises us first. We are too anxious about our supposedly too-thin lips to revise for our A levels, so consumed with how we look while having sex with a man we forget to ask ourselves whether we are enjoying it, or whether it even matters.

Wolf certainly wasn't the first to write about the tyranny of meeting unrealistic standards of beauty. The French existentialist Simone de Beauvoir wrote about the difficulties women face achieving freedom from societal expectations about appearance in her 1949 book *The Second Sex*:

> Since woman is an object, it is quite understandable that her intrinsic value is affected by her style of dress and adornment. It is not entirely futile for her to attach so much importance as she does to silk or nylon stockings, to gloves, to a hat, because it is an imperative obligation for her to keep up her position.

In the mid-2020s, the word adornment feels like an understatement. Almost everything about the way a woman looks is now examined and it has gone well beyond hats, gloves and stockings; even skin texture is a thing (less is better), as if every part of our natural body is wrong and needs smoothing out, or should even disappear altogether (think pores, fine lines and pubic hair). No wonder we see ourselves as Too Much when the beauty industry is trying to literally erase us with its so-called active ingredients. What I worry about is the sheer amount of time we spend on this shit, preventing us from seeing what's in front of our eyes (hypocrisy and injustice) and surrounding our eyes (completely normal skin, thanks very much). Then come the more obvious examples of the kind of restrictive conventions preventing us from acting freely that de Beauvoir described; for example heels, wearing the 'correct' length skirts, some religious clothing, extreme shapewear and dangerous uniforms not designed for the female body. How can we break free from these material prisons and resist spending so much of our leisure time on beauty work?

Not Just a Pretty Beard

There have been various attempts to encourage women to change the way they think about their bodies and appearance. The body positivity movement, popularised in recent years by mass social media and advertising, aims to accept and celebrate all bodies, regardless of shape, size and skin tone, at the same time as highlighting the ridiculous pressure facing women to look a certain way. The movement encourages individual women to love their bodies and to feel positive about them. Countless brands sell their products using #bodypositivity as the message. Much less commercially appealing is the idea of body neutrality. The idea is that your body is not something to love or celebrate, it just is. The body is functional and serves a purpose. In body neutrality your appearance doesn't matter at all and shouldn't be something you think about. Framed as a lifelong practice, feeling neither love nor hate for your body is something you achieve, working towards it by focusing on your values and what really matters to you. Depending on your starting point, you might do this alongside professional help from a therapist to help you to reframe your thoughts and counter excessive thoughts about your body.

The blurb for *Disobedient Bodies* by Emma Dabiri says that the book 'encourages unruliness, exploring the ways in which we can rebel against and subvert the current system. Offering alternative ways of seeing beauty, drawing on other cultures, worldviews, times, and places [...] to reconnect with our birthright and find the inherent joy in our disobedient bodies.' The blurb asks, 'What part of your beautiful self were you taught to hate?', arguing that 'We spend a lot of time trying to improve our "defects", according to society's ideals of beauty. But these ideals – which are often reductive, tyrannical and commercially entangled – are imposed upon us by oppressive systems and further strengthened by our conditioned self-loathing.' Absolutely, but body neutrality and Dabiri's call for disobedience place the onus on women, as individuals, to subvert the system, perhaps without recognising that these rebellious attitudes carry a huge personal cost in a patriarchal society. Younger women and those who look 'good for their age' may not see the point, noticing that they have an 'advantage' over other women, not realising that they too will grow old, as Victoria Smith explains in her book on the demonisation of middle-aged women, *Hags*. And by then, who is going to listen to them? Certainly not the younger women who can't see the problem, or don't want to look.

Furthermore, hating your body and trying to improve, or erase, it is an entirely rational response to a patriarchal, capitalist society that values youth and beauty in women. According to Dr Vivian Diller's book, *Face It: What Women Really Feel As Their Looks Change,* most women acknowledge that 'good looks continue to be associated with respect, legitimacy, and power in their relationships with others.' Diller concludes that in the workplace, where hiring and promotions are based on appearance, women are forced to prioritise what they look like above their actual work. When I talk about value here, I mean women's worth as judged by men, summarised so well by Smith in *Hags* as the three F's: feminine, fertile and fuckable. This may sound cynical, and of course this is not played out in every relationship, every workplace and every family dynamic, but this is where we learn our value lies. We learn it from boys at school judging our appearance and marking us out of ten. We overhear comments from our dads, grandads and brothers about women on TV and online. We are leered at in the street and shown porn by boys at school, or we find it ourselves, believing that the sex that happens in porn is how sex should be. Worse still, we learn our role in porn as POV objects to be consumed: passive, thin and humiliated. We watch adverts, films and videos, read books, follow influencers and listen to music that tell us how a woman should be. Taking all this together tells us to be highly body conscious, as if our lives depend on it, the very opposite of body neutral; more like #bodyobsessed.

All of this shit can be dismissed with a shrug of the shoulders and the expression 'sex sells'. But when we say this, we aren't talking about the image of a bald middle-aged man in his boxer shorts draped over a car, or two women in their seventies snogging on the sofa after *Strictly Come Dancing*. It means men of all ages consuming images of young women with nubile bodies. This is the lens, the male lens, the point of view through which, even if we reject it, we have been taught to see and judge ourselves and other women. We see ourselves as the view as Margot did in 'Cat Person'. Add to this companies telling us we have problems (parched hair? pigmented skin? open pores?) that even Basil Fawlty couldn't have dreamed of in his nastiest moments, and no wonder we clamour to buy the solutions (keratin hair treatment, retinol 2 per cent, charcoal mask).

Flipping Patriarchy

Meanwhile, as Philippa Perry's husband, Grayson Perry, writes in *The Descent of Man*, boys and men are gifted the body-neutral perspective, with their choice of clothing limited to just a few standard colours (black, blue, red and grey), the ideal look being either sportswear or something resembling the sort of uniform required to carry out traditional men's work. Put simply, men's clothing is functional, practical or, when branded or good quality, signals status. For men over thirty, a shirt and jeans will do, within the narrow range of acceptable colours and patterns. Another man talking about men's issues is the ever-strident Stewart Lee, who says in one of his stand-up routines that, like most men, he doesn't know where his pants came from. Smirking Stewart can't remember buying a single pair, even though he has plenty.[2] This will be because his mother, girlfriend or wife bought them for him, a phenomenon de Beauvoir wrote about without conceit and not for laughs in 1949:

> Man hardly has to take thought of his clothes, for they are convenient, suitable to his active life, not necessarily elegant; they are scarcely a part of his personality. More, nobody expects him to take care of them himself; some kindly disposed or hired female relative relieves him of the bother.

More than seventy years after de Beauvoir wrote this and nothing has changed in this department. We laugh at Lee's undercrackers gag because it's true, not just because it's about pants. Whether or not Stewart Lee was describing his own pants situation is irrelevant; it's a reminder that whatever lefty men say or write about equality for likes or laughs, they show who they really are at home. So men are literally gifted their underwear (and often the rest of their clothes), meaning no decision-making or thinking is required. Their clothes magically arrive in their wardrobes and drawers, delivered by the woman-fairy. This relative neutrality frees men up to do other stuff, including enjoying more brain space for work, and more free time. And that's on top of the free time men are apparently naturally entitled to, to pursue their very important hobbies, such as cycling, running and going to the gym.

No wonder women are exhausted. And no wonder married men are happier. As Michael Caine, now in his nineties, advised, one of his three secrets to a long and happy life is to 'take a younger wife.'[3] No mention of whether the taken wives have a long and happy life, or perhaps they don't matter, existing only in relation to the default male.

So while at an individual level we can work hard at taking a neutral, positive and accepting stance towards our bodies and becoming disobedient in the face of pressure to look a certain way, I can't help feeling this is the equivalent to being an atheist in relation to the existence of God. If we believe in the perfect female body (like believing in God), then neutrality, disobedience and body positivity are rejections of this belief. I agree that these movements encourage us to take a more biological, sane and individual approach to our bodies: a natural reaction against the status quo. However, body neutrality, positivity and the idea of disobedience still exist in relation to the cult of female beauty and perfection. To extend the belief metaphor, perhaps we could borrow from the humanist approach to the world when thinking about our response. As Dr Alice Roberts explained on Radio 4's *Desert Island Discs* when she was president of Humanists UK, humanists do not define themselves by what they don't believe in. Instead, they are positive about what they do believe in, and that is understanding the world through science. I would advocate a similar positive approach here. Perhaps the best we can do if we want to become an equal subject (rather than the object) is to focus on what we do stand for: our values and our purpose in life. Our inner life. No particular hashtag, journal or outerwear necessary.

I paint a dismal picture of the state we are in: women #bodyobsessed while men couldn't give a toss. One more area of inequality to add to the heap, with no clear way out. It seems unlikely women of the 2020s will be burning their false eyelashes, nails and hair extensions (imagine the smell!) in a symbolic act of liberation, like feminists of the 1960s burned their bras. It feels like the narrative of individual choice (just don't buy beauty products, then) and women looking pretty for themselves or for other women is too entrenched. Nor will there be an amnesty of beauty products where women surrender viral cosmetics they'll never use to the Head Feminist: concealers, foundations, primers, serums, illuminators and other potions that promise to make everything alright. I wonder what she would do with such an enormous stash. Make them into a giant, glossy, gloopy soup, visible from the moon, and exhibit said soup in a museum? *This is what women used to put on their faces*, the information board would say. After the exhibition closed, the fantasy face syrup could be offered to men in need of a subtle wash of colour to even skin tone and brighten the complexion (apply with a damp sponge, taking care not to drag product across the delicate under-eye area). Looks like he put it on with a trowel, the women would say.

Another less visceral and temporary solution is that women married to, or in partnerships with, men should at least be able to buy all the aforementioned shite (if they feel the need to buy it, as I and many others do) from the joint account. Because the beauty load is a tax on women, affecting our mental health, robbing us of time and wasting our money. Men are largely free from the cost, effort and disappointment of the whole sorry business. #bodyneutrality is an appealing way out, but it would have to be adopted on a mass scale, with a major shift from cosmetic companies, influencers and retailers towards the design of functional clothes and intelligent products for women's bodies, definitely with pockets. This would replace the current emphasis on women as purely decorative and light-reflecting objects. Going further, until women are free from male oppression (set timer on phone), we could treat the beauty burden on women as a public health issue. Governments could step in to treat viral products as outbreaks, offering support to those women whose mental health is affected (many of us), with much wider and tighter regulation of the beauty industry, recognising that cult products emanate from an actual cult, where nearly all the victims are women.

The solution, of course, has to be much bigger, involving deeper sacrifice, tackling weightier issues, huge societal shifts, changed norms and expectations of the sort authors like Laura Bates write about in *Fix the System, Not the Women*. All I can do in my book is mock this particular and very visible aspect of the patriarchy, shining a light on the gendered burden on women. If reading this chapter encourages one more woman to lay down her eyelash serum, worry less about her thigh gap and read more feminist books, then I won't be happy. Because it cannot be an individual responsibility, what with that massive fuck-off to-do list we have to get through. The beauty load is a consequence of the patriarchal society we live in, not a personal choice we can easily opt out of. We are not shallow or vain; we are intelligent and rational. Economic Woman, if you like, and I certainly do. So as you were, women – none of this is your fault, keep applying the serum, looking for the perfect coat and checking your face in the mirror. Don't change a thing. You are perfect just as you are.

The Beauty Load

- Stay young
- Be fertile, feminine and fuckable
- Be an object
- Be invisible but luminous
- And don't forget to smile!

4.

Heard the One About a Man Trying to Park a Car?

It was the mid-2010s and I was at a celebrity fundraising dinner wearing a black Topshop wrap dress and heels, my attempt to look like someone happy in her own skin. Unfortunately, I felt self-conscious and vulnerable, worrying I might fall over and unwrap at any moment; scared to stand on my own feet. Relieved once seated, I settled into the wine and speech, delivered by an average male sports presenter. Keen to connect with the audience, he told a series of one-liners, including mother-in-law jokes, blonde jokes and wife jokes. The message behind these jokes was that women are either fuckable and stupid or old and annoying and should probably stay in the kitchen, be silent or dead. As he cheerfully spewed forth, I looked around and saw people, women and men, even teenagers, laughing with their heads tilting back, faces flushed with pleasure. They clearly had great affection for this family entertainer. Except for my boss, an older, more confident woman, actually happy in her own skin. She had a non-laughing face, unmoved by his 'jokes'.

We glanced at each other and she raised her eyebrows. After

Mr Presenter finished his very funny speech, fuelled by free Prosecco, I suggested she might want to go and have a word with him about his jokes. *Go on, go on, go on.* Egged on, she did, and I followed, standing behind her like a dog waiting outside a shop. I strained to listen as she asked politely if he thought sexist jokes were appropriate for a family audience. Clearly annoyed and only receptive to fawning praise, he didn't thank her. Instead, his reaction made my boss want to leave quickly. I heard nothing more about it, but I admired her courage and made a mental note – this is what happens when you challenge sexist jokes. It is you who leaves the room.

Woman-hating fun

So there we are. Woman-hating was, and often still is, seen as appropriate for all ages. And not only that, the source of the mockery is enthusiastically applauded. Yes, that's right, clapping hate is family entertainment. Just a bit of fun, only having a laugh, don't be so uptight, what's your problem? Everyone else is laughing, you're reading too much into it, don't bring the mood down, you're the real sexist, CAN'T YOU TAKE A JOKE?

Bringing the mood down further are the studies showing that a man's exposure to sexist jokes is linked to his rape proclivity, i.e. how likely he is to rape a woman.[1] Unsurprisingly, woman-hating humour makes it easier for men who already have unpleasant attitudes towards women to express their biases without fear of any consequences. And if everyone is laughing and clapping along with you, not only is sexism consequence-free, it's positively encouraged. This makes misogynistic humour an important part of the patriarchy, and one that is highly resistant to change. Attempts to challenge the teller or sharer of a sexist gag are usually met with hostility, with accusations that the pointer-outer is the real problem. At best the joker may concede you have a point, but they will quickly tell you that there is a better, nicer way to go about it; in other words, shut up.

Most of us have heard jokes mocking mothers-in-law, 'dumb blondes' and female drivers. Some of us have probably laughed at them. Google 'mother-in-law jokes' and one result boasts several thousand to choose from. Search 'father-in-law jokes' and the top result is 'How come you never hear father-in-law jokes?' I can answer that! Because sexism. An alternative search suggested by Google is 'father-in-law one-liners'. The algorithm knows that as a rule of thumb (or penis), men, fathers-in-law in this case, *tell* the jokes, as part of a father-of-the-bride speech for example. Women, on the other hand, are more likely to be the objects of them.

Still popular at weddings, in after-dinner speeches, in changing rooms, on Facebook, Reddit and WhatsApp groups, sexist jokes are presented as harmless, inevitable and natural when a group of men get together. For the so-called biological explanation (and justification) see cavemen and apes. The apparently gender-neutral and harmless joke categories 'adult', 'pick-up' and 'dirty' are particularly unpleasant. There is, of course, nothing neutral about them. They are overwhelmingly jokes written and told by men with women as the punchline, treated as body parts, wives, servants and fuckables. This type of humour would be more accurately categorised as anti-women or woman-hating.

Flipping Patriarchy

The switcheroo

The collection of gags that follow reverse these boresome tropes, holding a mirror up to a culture that laughs at, belittles and sexualises women for fun. Imagine if men were the objects of sexist humour in popular culture, instead of women. This collection of gags turns traditional sexist jokes on their head, making men the punchline. If you are thinking, but what about sexist jokes against men? Surely women get together and joke about their husbands? They do, but hold your horses, I'll cover this later.

The gender-flipped jokes are all inspired by real-world internet sources, you can find links to them at the end of this book in the Inspired By section.

So imagine as you read the gags that you are listening to Claire, my boss from ten years ago, deliver them in her speech to a family audience on the day of her wedding. Think of how she is introduced: as The Woman, The Myth, The Legend. The guests stand up before she has uttered a word. They know they are in for a treat. They love a woman's woman, a woman who is not afraid to tell it how it is.

Gentleman and ladies, boys and girls. A wise friend told me this speech will be my last opportunity to talk without being nagged or scolded, so I hope you are sitting comfortably because I'm going to make the most if it! I am so lucky to have married Liam. My mother congratulated me last Friday in fact, saying, 'Claire, mark my words, this will be the happiest day of*

---

* Claire thinks it should always be gentlemen first because it's good manners, and also because she likes to look at their arses as they pass in front of her.

102

Heard the One About a Man Trying to Park a Car?

your life.' Absolutely, I thought, as I left the house for my hen do.

On the first day, God created light and darkness and rested. On the second day, God created the sky and rested. On the third day, God created land and rested. On the fourth day, God created the sun and the moon and rested. On the fifth day, God created birds and animals and rested. On the sixth day, God created woman and rested. Then God created man, and ever since neither God nor woman has rested!

Claire's hilarious speech continues with a string of one-liners from her well-thumbed joke book, *Best Eyebrow-Raising Jokes of All Time!* The blurb on the back cover promises to sort the women from the girls and guarantees a raised eyebrow from the menfolk!

The fictional book is split by category so you can easily find a joke on any topic. Here are some of Claire's favourites:

Father-in-law jokes

I always remember a face. But in my father-in-law's case, I try not to.

Karen said, 'My father-in-law is a saint.' Susan replied, 'You're blessed. Mine is still living!'

My father-in-law's second car is a broomstick!

I went to Madame Tussauds' Chamber of Horrors with my elderly father-in-law. One of the staff said to me, 'Don't let him stand still, madam, we're archiving.'

Flipping Patriarchy

My father-in-law has terrible hay fever and high cholesterol . . . On special occasions, I gift him flowers and chocolates.

What's the penalty for having two husbands? Two fathers-in-law!

Blond jokes

What's the best way to make a blond man laugh on a Thursday? Tell him a joke on Monday.

A blond man asks the baker for a cake. She replies, 'How many slices would you like me to cut it into? Four, six or ten?' The blond says, 'Four please, I could never eat ten.'

On the drive to Alton Towers, three blond men see a sign on the motorway saying ALTON TOWERS LEFT. So the three men burst into tears and drive home.

Four blond men walk into a shop. I'm surprised not one of them saw it!

I was in the supermarket recently and saw a blond man gazing at a bottle of fabric conditioner. I was curious, so I asked him why he was so fixated with it and he replied, 'The label says "concentrate"'.

Heard the One About a Man Trying to Park a Car?

A blond man called 999 to report that his shop was on fire. The operator asked him how to get to his shop. The blond replied, 'In your fire engine!'

When a blond man wakes up in the morning, what does he do first? He gets out of my bed, puts his clothes on and goes home.

How many blond men does it take to screw in a light bulb? Blond men don't screw in light bulbs; they screw in car parks.

What's the best way to get a blond to go home with you? Ask him.

How can you tell a dog and a blond apart? Training a dog only takes a few weeks.

Male driver jokes

Some men eventually turn into good drivers. So if you're a driver, look out!

How is it that male drivers are so terrible at using their indicators? Because they are so used to giving women mixed signals.

My first husband's incessant whining became too much, and divorce costs a fortune, so I sent him out to reverse into a parking space. I've heard on the grapevine he's still trying, lurching this way and that. God bless him.

When a woman drives her car into a man, who is to blame? Erm . . . why exactly was the woman driving a car in the kitchen?

What easily fills six parking spaces? Two male drivers.

What's another word for a decent male driver? A fantasy!

Kitchen jokes

What's the best way to repair a gentleman's watch? You don't bother; there's a timepiece on the oven.

When your husband leaves the kitchen, what does this tell you? His lead isn't short enough!

What do men quarrel over when they play Monopoly? Who gets to use the iron.

Why do no men live on the moon? Because the moon doesn't need ironing.

Husband jokes

For forty years after my husband passed away I didn't meet another man. Then I was released from prison and I made up for it!

What's the definition of marriage for a woman? A costly way to get your housework done for free.

A wise woman once declared, 'I didn't know what true contentment was until we got married, and by that time it was too late.'

What's another word for a man whose mental capacity has been reduced by 95 per cent? A widower.

What happens just before a man says something intelligent? He starts by saying, 'A woman explained to me. . .'

What's the best way for a woman to learn the date of her wedding anniversary? To fail to remember it once.

Dirty jokes

How do you make a man horny? You do his laundry.

How do you know if your husband has died? The sex stays the same, but no one cleans the bathroom.

I prefer my men to be like my laptop: a nice display; on my knee; virus free.

How are dog poo and men the same? The longer they've been around, the easier they are to pick up.

The best eyebrow-raising jokes of all time end, and the speech closes. The audience are on their feet again. They loved the risqué jokes from charismatic Claire, a larger-than-life character with a colourful past. Everyone agrees she is a marvellous compère, except two men. They aren't laughing. One of them has a word with her afterwards as the other waits nervously behind him. Claire contemplates the younger one's figure as she listens to the older man. She hasn't come all the way into the city for an earful, she says, when she can get that at home. The women around her laugh loudly. The two men leave with their hearts racing, burning with the injustice and humiliation. Claire sits back with a whisky and checks out their bums as they walk back to their table. She takes a sip and decides that she would. Those boys need to be taught a lesson.

Claire and her mates go to a ladies' club for a couple more drinks, where the banter continues and the hilarious 'your dad' insults begin . . .

Your dad's so fat

Your dad's so fat, it took me two trains and a taxi to get around to his better side.

Your dad's so fat, when he orders fish and chips at the seaside, the seagulls hide their food.

Your dad's so fat, when I veered sideways to avoid knocking him over, my van nearly ran out of fuel.

Heard the One About a Man Trying to Park a Car?

Your dad's so fat, when he stood near the window the sun went in.

Your dad's so fat, even his bike has stretch marks.

Your dad's so fat, he can't even jump at an opportunity.

Your dad's so ugly

Your dad's so ugly, when he threw a ball for a dog, it refused to come back.

Your dad's so ugly, he went on a ghost train and came out with a job offer.

Your dad's so ugly, even his reflection looks away.

Your dad's so ugly, he could make a King's Guard cry.

Your dad's so stupid

Your dad's so stupid, when the judge said, 'Order!' your dad asked for chicken and chips.

Your dad's so stupid, he got hit by a stationary vehicle.

Your dad's so stupid, when I told him he'd lost his marbles, he tried to find them.

Your dad's so stupid, when burglars stole his phone, he raced after them screaming, 'Stop, you forgot the charger!'

Your dad's so stupid, he peered around a glass door to find out what was on the other side.

Your dad's so stupid, he took a ruler on a marathon to measure the race.

Who's laughing now?

When you put the shoe on the other foot, how do men feel? Is it still just a bit of fun? Can you take a joke? Who's laughing now?

Not me, actually. Although all the jokes are an obvious switcheroo, I still find the Claire scenario and the gags relentlessly grim and unfunny. They certainly make me think, but they don't make me laugh. In these 'jokes', we apparently want fathers-in-law dead, all blond men are stupid, men can't drive, husbands are good for one thing only and your dad is fat, ugly and stupid. Taking them at face value, I don't find them funny because they don't connect, they don't build on or reinforce what I have been conditioned to think. There is no knowing laugh or smug recognition. Unlike the studies about rape proclivity, I do not already have unpleasant attitudes towards men. I love my father-in-law, I know hair colour doesn't affect men's intelligence and I don't want my husband to do my ironing. I can do my own.

Heard the One About a Man Trying to Park a Car?

Women have very little idea of how much men hate them
Reversing the jokes reveals the hatred and contempt for women at large in 'good ol'-fashioned humour'. The apparent crimes women commit are made obvious: old, fat, ugly, stupid, blonde, married, driving, being a mum or having a mum.

As Germaine Greer famously observed in the 1970 classic *The Female Eunuch*: 'Women have very little idea of how much men hate them.' We do have an idea when we read these gender-flipped jokes, one after another. And there is no escape from the vitriol. Young women become old women, girlfriends turn into wives, daughters turn into mothers and then mothers-in-law. And this is the point: existing as a woman is, in itself, apparently too much. As a woman, you are fair game for ridicule and contempt, regardless of the sub-category allocated to you. Note that the category of fully rounded, interesting and complex human is not available, and would probably be classed as a joke in itself.

Men have very little idea of how much women respect them
I can hear the response, 'But don't women laugh at men? What about all those jokes about men having small penises? Don't women get together in groups and joke about how useless their husbands are?' The answer is yes, but the jokes and the context in which they are shared are not equivalent. The hate is absent. I am yet to meet a woman who hates men. There is no culture of man-hating amongst women. Instead, we treat men as people, and with respect, deserved or not.

The jokes women tell and the banter we share tends to be observational, laughing in recognition of a shared experience, much of it borne from disappointment or despair. The jokes below, categorised online as 'sexist jokes against men', are the same.

What do birthdays, the Hoover and the G-spot all have in common? Men can't locate any of them.

What do husbands and printers have in common? They're expensive to run and only function half the time.

Husband: Do you fancy a quick shag?
Wife: As an alternative to what?

How many gentlemen does it take to change a light bulb? One. A man just holds it in his hand and waits for the light fitting to come to him.

How are men and long-term savings accounts different? Long-term savings accounts get better with age.

Men are like fixed-rate bonds; with enough money, they are guaranteed to get interest.

These jokes reinforce stereotypes about men being immature, selfish breadwinners. Far from being anti-men, these jokes actually maintain stereotypes that serve the patriarchy and maintain the status quo. The jokes do not attack or dehumanise. They are not punching down. Claiming that women make

Heard the One About a Man Trying to Park a Car?

sexist jokes is false equivalence. It does not bear up to scrutiny. The two sets of jokes when compared may look similar to an alien or to an artificial intelligence system. But I would hope we can see past the superficial similarity and realise we do not live in an artificial world free from power and context. Unlike AI, we can go deeper and see the logical fallacy. The retort, 'But women tell sexist jokes against men!' is used as a deliberate distraction from the issue at hand, a mistaken belief known as 'whataboutism'. This fallacy, combined with false equivalence, produces the following claim: 'You're saying that sexist jokes against women (*linked to rape, reinforcing male power, normalised, frequent*) are bad, but *what about* the (*relatively minor, infrequent and tame*) jokes women tell about men?' The only word I see equivalent here is 'jokes'. It is false to claim further equivalence.

I understand that the jokes above may *feel* sexist to men, but I would go further than the phrase 'To those accustomed to privilege, equality feels like oppression' and suggest that to those accustomed to privilege, saying anything at all about sexism, even if said in a whisper, in italics or with a smiley face, feels like oppression. The truth is that man-hating humour does not exist in popular culture or in private conversations between friends. Women do not routinely show their hatred and contempt for men through humour, because there is no hate and contempt to show. If you use the 'women are just as bad as men' argument as a defence for actual sexist jokes built on actual woman-hating, you're having a laugh.

Men have very little idea of how much women fear them

Attributed to Margaret Atwood is the famous quote: 'Men are afraid that women will laugh at them. Women are afraid that men will kill them.' We can see that one of these fears is rather more serious than the other. Imagine only being afraid that a man will laugh at you! No more planning your route home, being careful about what you say or being worried about meeting a Tinder date. Instead, your greatest fear might be a gaggle of drunk men on a stag do laughing at your hair. I would happily take on the worry of a man mocking the size of my feet over the fear of him killing me.

Women are of course rationally afraid of both being killed and laughed at, because the two are connected. Sexist jokes and men mocking a woman's age or weight, for example, are part of the same patriarchal society where male violence flourishes. The jokes are a reminder of who is in charge and of our place in the world.

Another more subtle reminder of who calls the shots is the more serious form of humour called satire.

The purpose of satire

Satire, according to the *Oxford English Dictionary*, is supposed to be the use of humour, irony, exaggeration or ridicule to expose and criticise people's stupidity or vices, particularly in the context of contemporary politics and other topical issues. But, like every other field, especially the fun ones, satire is dominated by those in power, particularly men. As the late author and satirist Terry Pratchett said: 'Satire is meant to

Heard the One About a Man Trying to Park a Car?

ridicule power. If you are laughing at people who are hurting, it's not satire, it's bullying.'[2]

Now for some actual satire, on satire itself. Let's imagine that men's satire is a Thing; a tradition and a category with its own shelf in a library. Imagine academics studying this niche genre. The following text is a gender-flipped excerpt from an actual academic article on women satirists.

This oversight of men satirists is grounded in the taboo against men expressing aggression in literature and that 'the position of the male writer already rendered precarious by its deviation from the norm, is exacerbated by his position as satirist and as man.'

In most criticism of satirical writers, men are treated as anomalies within the genre, individually compared with female satirists but never juxtaposed with other men.

While female satirists establish themselves as superior, 'defining, controlling, dealing out the analyses that hurt, dishing out the critical medicine' to the society which they critique, male satirists wield their caustic pen from a distance that is on the fringe rather than from a 'privileged height'. They know that if they make their accusations too blatant then they risk being further marginalized by the matriarchal society which they are critiquing. They disguise their barbs so that the objects of their satire will find them more agreeable, and it is this temperance of their aggression that allows the barbs to penetrate deeper into society than a more obvious attack might.

Despite the abundance of scholarship about satire produced

Flipping Patriarchy

within the past decade, men's satire is an area that has been largely ignored. One reason why there are so few studies about men's satire is that men theorists and critics distance themselves from the genre, making the argument that satire and men's writing are in contention with one another.

Furthermore, men's satire uses humour and an emphasis on the subjective experiences of men to deflate the feminine focus on empiricism, objectivity and literary exclusivity.[3]

Wow. Men as a deviation of the norm, on the fringe, being ignored and marginalised, disguising their barbs, being too blatant and treated as anomalies. Unimaginable, isn't it?

The problem with satire

Taking Terry Pratchett's definition about satire ridiculing power, you would think that a pivotal part of satire would be to mock the patriarchy, given it is arguably the most persistent system of power across the world. And yet some of the most prominent and long-running UK TV satirical shows, *Have I Got News for You* and *Mock the Week*, Radio 4's *The News Quiz* and the magazine *Private Eye*, appear to have a blind spot when it comes to ripping into male power. No one gives a toss.

Why might this be? Could it be that the majority of producers, presenters and guests are men who benefit from the patriarchy? These are the men who decide where to punch and which hypocrisies to puncture. Popular themes for men satirists to have a pop at are government, the royal family and royals, religion, popular culture, the wealthy elite and even comedy itself. Punching up here is well-worn territory, and

Heard the One About a Man Trying to Park a Car?

there is certainly plenty to go around. But the patriarchy? Nope, hardly a peep.

In Satire VI, from the late first century, Juvenal wrote: 'A man will never be happy while his mother-in-law lives; she teaches her daughter evil habits.' While this may have been viewed as a satirical statement of the times, hilariously comparing the morality of women of the past to modern Roman women, in no sense does it ridicule actual power, and this early satire sets a pattern. We mock the world, the week and the news through the male lens. Meanwhile, men's morality and fathers-in-law go unscrutinised. The patriarchy enjoys near protected status in mainstream satire, and in comedy more generally, past and present.

At an event in 2019, male comedian Steve Coogan claimed the following:

> I never punch down [...] If I satirise or attack anyone it's the powerful [...] Comedy is actually one of the few things, if you do it properly, you can talk about difficult things and you can point out hypocrisies about things [...] Even in terms of sexual politics.[4]

I agree with Mr Coogan. Mocking male power, which I hope is part of his more ambiguous and equal-sounding label 'sexual politics', feels almost off-limits, a difficult thing you can't actually talk about. And that's a problem. Male satirists, the ones hogging the TV shows and the stand-up circuit, tend to poke fun where they experience injustice, especially on a personal level. But not everyone is a middle-aged man who

Flipping Patriarchy

didn't go to public school and pokes fun at those who did. There must be something else we can laugh at.

Common targets for male satirists tend to be other more powerful men, as Coogan identifies: politicians, celebrities or other public figures. So while men become targets through their actions or status, women are fair game simply because they are women. Professor of English at Syracuse University Felicity Nussbaum writes, 'The target of much satire is female as a sex.'[5]

Another professor, Paul Simpson from the University of Liverpool, agrees:

> A deeply misogynistic practice in canonical satirical writing where, while males become targets through their individuality, women feature only by dint of their gender. Few if any of the distinctions that are made for men are afforded to women and this results in the female becoming 'a metaphor for all that is threatening and offensive to society' (Nussbaum 1984: 19–20).[6]

Meanwhile, because men don't experience sexism in all its wretched daily detail, they have no anecdotes and zero material, even if they wanted to tackle it. And so there remains a big steaming pile of it, untouched by human hand and ripe for mockery.

Who can take on this important job? Which large group of people might be uniquely qualified to hold this particular form of power to account? Is it the same male jokers who are happy to take on the class system but can't resist the odd mother-in-law joke? Or how about the male satirists who bravely take on dictators then minutes later think it is similarly brave to joke about raping famous women. Or might it be the male 'alternative' comedians from the 1980s, who apparently break with traditional comedy but keep a little bit of sexism back for themselves as a treat? Nope. None of this is satire. It is, as Terry Pratchett said, bullying. Or, as I say, woman-hating. Same old shit.

Proper satire

The real alternative comedy comes from women, especially feminists and those unafraid to tell it how it is, skewering prejudice, exposing hypocrisy and puncturing the vanity of the patriarchy. These are the jokes that have the power to truly shock and be genuinely alternative. They also have the potential to appeal to over half of the population. So where are the mainstream TV and radio comedy shows ridiculing sexists, mocking so-called banter and cat-calling, laughing at mansplainers, calling out rape 'jokes' and exposing everyday sexism? How can this not be a mainstay of satire?

There are a whole load of brilliant comedians who do exactly this, for example Amy Schumer, and her brilliant 2015 sketch 'Last Fuckable Day'. A group of famous women – Amy Schumer, Tina Fey, Julia Louis-Dreyfus and Patricia Arquette – are celebrating a very special occasion: Julia's Last Fuckable Day. The sketch satirises the way women are judged in the media as believably fuckable or not, the last fuckable day therefore being a turning point in a woman's life. This of course resonates beyond the media to a societal view of a woman's value, and in turn the way a woman values herself. As the sketch suggests, there are advantages to being no

Flipping Patriarchy

longer seen as fuckable, the freedom to not care about your appearance being one. But this is a consolation prize, not a win. The real prize would be not having any fucks to give in the first place. Also highlighted in the sketch is the double standard. There is no Last Fuckable Day for men.

Another phenomenal satirical sketch is Rachel Parris's 2022 take on male violence, 'Women Are Knackered', on the *Late Night Mash* show. What makes this sequence particularly special is that her co-star, male comedian Nish Kumar, is the foil, while Parris is the star. She opens by asking Kumar with feigned curiosity if, when he hears women talking about the epidemic of male violence, he feels the urge to immediately step in and say, 'It wasn't me.' Kumar replies with a confused 'No, not really.' She replies explaining that this is because 'actually, you're not a prick', to audience laughter. She also mocks former MP Dominic Raab for thinking 'misogyny is of course completely wrong, whether it's a man against a woman or a woman against a man', because, as she says, 'It is tricky to know the meaning of a word that affects 51 per cent of the population. I mean, what you do expect him to do, look it up?' The name of the sketch, 'Women are Knackered', refers to the overall theme, which satirises the view that it is women's responsibility to tackle male violence.

An earlier satirical take on male power and privilege is Judy Brady's essay 'I Want a Wife', printed in *Ms.* magazine in 1971.[7] Tongue-in-cheek, Judy asks for a wife:

I want a wife who will keep my house clean.

Heard the One About a Man Trying to Park a Car?

She wants a wife to do all the things; not only the practical things, but to take on the emotional load, too:

> I want a wife who will listen to me when I feel the need to explain a rather difficult point I have come across in my course of studies.

And she wants a wife to take care of her sexual needs:

> I want a wife who is sensitive to my sexual needs . . . a wife who makes sure that I am satisfied.

The essay ends with the question, 'My god, who wouldn't want a wife?' And over fifty years later, this question remains. Women are still joking that what they really need is a wife, and most actually mean it. I certainly do.

Amy Schumer, Rachel Parris and Judy Brady, along with many other legendary comedians – Sophie Duker, Hannah Gadsby, Sasheer Zamata, Aisha Brown, Katherine Ryan, Bridget Christie, Sofie Hagen, Kate Smurthwaite, Sara Pascoe, Rosie Holt, Lindy West, Lou Sanders, Aisling Bea, Jo Brand, Diane Morgan, Ellie Taylor, Lucy Porter, Eleanor Morton and Alice Fraser (I could fill a book with names) – do everything satire is supposed to be about. Holding power to account.

So imagine we have a bit of a changeround, and we invite these women to look after the mainstream comedy shows, the ones people actually watch. Imagine women hosting late-night American television shows on their own for the next few decades, centuries maybe. Imagine (reversing some

Flipping Patriarchy

actual statistics) women earning 60 per cent more than men at the Edinburgh Fringe.[8] Imagine just 11 per cent of TV comedy shows being written by men.[9] Add to this the fantasy that these women aren't afraid of telling difficult jokes, ones that may be offensive to men's vanities.

Imagine Steve Coogan pitching a comedy programme to the BBC and it being rejected on the basis that they already have a sitcom with men in it.[*]

Meanwhile, imagine the men comedians getting together to do their own male-themed shows during the annual regional Men in Comedy Festival or on International Men's Day. One male comic (tops) would be included on shows such as *QI*, *The Sports Quiz* and *Would I Lie to You?*, for balance (and as long as they only laugh at the real comedians and tell self-deprecating jokes about their weight and appearance). The producer of *Mock the Week* would lament the sad fact that although she charitably invites men comedians onto her show, they always turn it down because they don't want to be the token male. Shame.

Imagine a Wikipedia page titled 'Men in comedy':

> Men in comedy refers to men who participate in comedic works. The common perception that men aren't funny pervades all aspects of comedy, including stand-up, television and movies. The comedy establishment, influenced by matriarchal society, has relegated men to the side of tears and loss.

---

[*] When Caitlin Moran pitched *Raised by Wolves* to the BBC, it was rejected on the basis that they'd 'already got a sitcom with women in'.

Heard the One About a Man Trying to Park a Car?

A sense of humour in men was previously thought to have meant the ability to laugh at a woman's joke, rather than tell the joke himself. When men did finally enter comedy, it was seen as niche, thus making bookings hard to come by.

Early acts were often based in the standard roles of men as husbands and fathers. Comedy was tailored to what women would find to be both funny and non-threatening. As women slowly accepted a male presence in comedy, men were able to expand the topics that they covered. For male stand-up comedians, the direct contact with the audience puts their manhood on display. Many male comedians choose to wear loose-fitting trousers to take their masculinity out of the spotlight.

The early male figures in stand-up were able to enter the mainstream through their willingness to self-deprecate and declare themselves ugly, old or fat. Other early male comedians used sex appeal to attract audiences. In other words, they were able to enter, but not on the terms of proper comedians. More modern male comedians cite a need to tailor their comedy to what men themselves would find to be funny, with this change in mentality only coming very recently.[10]

It's funny cos it's not true. It's funny because it's the opposite. Your chapterly reminder that reversing what's true for laughs is what this book is about.

If you are a man reading this chapter and you have taken offence, please remember I am only joking. Really, I am. Just a bit of fun, only having a laugh, don't be so uptight, what's

Flipping Patriarchy

your problem? Everyone else is laughing, you're reading too much into it, don't bring the mood down, you're the real sexist, CAN'T YOU TAKE A JOKE?

Humour Load

- Challenge sexist jokes, even if this may damage your career or put you in danger
- Challenge sexist jokes in a nicer, better way (i.e. not at all)
- Become a satirist or a comedian
- Watch comedy written by women
- And don't forget to smile!

5.

Men in Sport

Remember, girls, you can be anything: a woman footballer, a lady cricketer, a podium girl, a token attractive female cyclist, a ball girl, one of the hottest female golfers of the year, a girl on a bike, a gorgeous fan in the crowd wearing a tight shirt, a tour host, an administrator, a fat-bottomed girl on a bike, the hot wife or girlfriend of an athlete or a semi-naked beach volleyball player 'glistening like a wet otter'.[1]

You can be anything, as long as you are attractive, young and playing a supporting role. And when I say attractive, I mean in a small, weak and slender way, not too fit, definitely not muscly and absolutely no big shoulders. Think hot, sexy and glowing. Playing competitive sport does not exempt you from Victoria Smith's three F's: fertile, feminine and fuckable.

Because, you see, sport is for men; it's the one thing they have left, if you don't count politics, business, music, science, religion and the arts. As Anna Kessel says in her podcast *The Game Changers*, this powerful and influential sphere is not a space for girls and women:

I just think, if you grow up as a girl, it's like there's a room in your house that you're not allowed to go in. That's how I see sport in life. There's a sphere in the world that is hugely powerful and influential, that political leaders fall over themselves to get involved with, and women are obstructed from that space. I think we cannot live a whole and complete life, we cannot play a full role in society, as long as that's the case.[2]

In this chapter, let's imagine a different room, one that boys are not allowed to go in, a room filled with girl's things: camaraderie, identity, pride, trophies, skill, competition, excitement, adrenaline, belonging, power, esteem, banter and money. A room where throwing like a boy is seen as an insult; the worst possible thing. A room where the women go to get away from the men. A sign on the door of the room says 'Keep Out'.

Much of what follows in this chapter is inspired by real-world events; you can find the sources in the Inspired By section at the back of the book.

Football

In this imaginary room, the girls know everything about football, the names of the highest earners, players and managers. They impress friends and relatives with their knowledge of statistics. They know the goal scorers, the height of players and upcoming fixtures. They play football in the garden, in the street and at school. When the girls were babies their mums and grandmas said they kicked like little footballers. And it started from there. The babygrows, T-shirts, birthday cakes, birthday cards and bedrooms all adorned with footballs. Football mad, she is.

All the little girls know who Helen Finch is, the (imaginary) chief executive of the Premier League (the Premier League, not the Men's Premier League). Finch is a role model for little girls, so grown-up, authoritative and powerful with her silver hair, fast cars and expensive suits. The mums talk about her football talent when she played for Manchester United as a young woman. No one mentions the rumours – it was a long time ago now. The dads don't approve; they tell their daughters she's a gentleman's woman. Which just adds to the excitement. 'When I grow up, I want to be like Finchy,' the little girls tell their teachers.

In her spare time, Finch is a committed champion of men's and boys' football. She has four boys of her own, a husband, two brothers, a dad and a male houseplant, so she definitely respects men and supports the men's game. What a lovely woman. A major story breaks, dominating the national news for days.

'Keep him off your vulva!' Vile emails exchanged between Premier League supremo Helen Finch and doctor pal

The head of the Premier League has been forced to apologise after a source revealed she sent a series of inappropriate emails from her work account.

Finch, a keen supporter of men's football, referred to males as

Flipping Patriarchy

'cock', mocked 'male irrationality' and told her doctor mate to keep a male colleague nicknamed Eddie 'off my vulva' in a series of crude emails.

Her views were today revealed by her former PA. He claims that his manager, who publicly backs men's football, exchanged nasty emails with her executive colleagues in which males were referred to as 'meat'.

And in another she said: 'I had a boyfriend once called Double Decker . . . let me play upstairs, but his mother would come looking for you if you went below.' She also mocked 'male irrationality' and forwarded a gag from a pal about a man trying to park a car. Finch likes to be seen as a champion of men in the game.

A Premier League source told us: 'Helen Finch understands that her comments were inappropriate and ill-judged, but they were not meant to be shared widely. The quotes were taken out of context. Her love of men, and support of the men's agenda, men's football and men in general is writ large. No one respects men more than Helen.'

Finch, who has been chief of the Premier League since 2004, said in one email to the doctor and another colleague: 'You will learn over time that male irrationality increases exponentially depending on how many males join your family.'

Finch's insults come after a survey this year found more than two-thirds of men working in football have experienced discriminatory behaviour and abuse. Her former PA added: 'I think people should know about this woman's attitude to men and the emails she is prepared to send from her work address.'

One of the Football Association's leading officers for men's

Men in Sport

and boys' football claimed Finch's disgusting emails could 'put men off football' for life. He claimed that as a male football leader he was warned against talking to the press.

Shadow Minister for Men, Mr Ali Hassan, said: 'No one should use deeply insulting language like this. Football is a family game, with many men and children supporters, men players and male referees. It's time to kick offensive attitudes towards men and boys out of football.'

And Tory MP Terry Smith, an experienced FA football coach and manager of a boys' youth team, joined the band of critics. Master Smith, who sits on Parliament's Culture, Media and Sport Select Committee, said: 'It's disappointing at a time when she's trying to encourage more men to play football that she is using unfortunate and frankly abusive language like this. It's an unpleasant and toxic environment for a man to be involved in, either as a player or an official, and, while most people can take a joke, it's important that somebody who is promoting the men's game shouldn't be using this kind of terminology.'

The mums read the news on their phones. Big girls message each other. Little girls pick up the story from their sisters. The mums try not to laugh or repeat the rude words, especially around the po-faced dads. All the boys stay quiet. Some are confused. Will they grow up to be 'meat' and 'cock'? The mums say girls will be girls, give the poor woman a break, can't you see she's been hounded by the media? Think of her mental health. How do you think she's feeling right now? She's a human being too. The little girls and big girls take it all in from the comfort of their rooms.

International Survey of Attitudes to Men in Sports

Following a link in another newspaper article about Finch's antics reveals more about attitudes to men and boys in sport. The National Institute for Boys in Sport UK carried out a representative survey of 2,011 people across twenty-two sports, looking at opinions on a range of issues, from the role of male pundits to how often Brits watch men's sport on TV.

Survey respondents acknowledged that inequality exists within sport, with the majority of people agreeing this is the case. Interestingly, though, 90 per cent of men said there is inequality in sport, versus 34 per cent of women showing that men might be perceiving something that just isn't there.

Here is a snapshot of troubling views from the survey on the topic:

They can play beach volleyball; I don't mind watching that.

Most male sports are really poor quality.

There is a huge gulf in skill levels. The women are way better and deserve more money.

My local first team could beat the England Gentlemen's team quite easily.

Men get more than they deserve.

Men should play sport that is suited to them, like the egg and spoon race!

The advancement of the men's game has been forced upon people.

Whatever sport women are interested in, men will want to be involved too for some reason.

> *Men are beginning to take over, they are headlining a lot of programmes, mainly making stupid comments or laughing all the time.*
>
> *Men should not be paid anywhere near as much as female sports stars.*
>
> *Men are getting more now – they're getting special treatment!*

The grandmas read the findings from the survey and nod wisely; it's all true, they say, you can't deny it. The grandads don't read it; they are too busy in the kitchen scrubbing the pans the grandmas left in the sink to soak. The big girls say kindly that actually men's football is getting better, quickly adding they prefer to watch men play beach volleyball. A glance at the mums and they approve. Like mother, like daughter. The dads sigh. The boys say nothing.

One week later and the same paper publishes an update:

Helen Finch: no further action over filthy emails

The Premier League sent a strong message of support for its boss today, saying Helen Finch will face 'no further disciplinary action' for sending mucky emails.

All of the league's chairwomen gave Finch, 54, unconditional support over recent events – a move that will disappoint critics of the most powerful woman in English football. The joint statement cited Finch's 'previously untarnished' record, and the testimonies of young men working in the offices at the Premier League, all backing their chief executive.

The committee and clubs decided not to take the matter further after seeing evidence that the emails 'did include some remarks of a lower standard than we would expect', but that Finch had apologised.

The investigation into Finch was carried out by Sheila Flannagan, the acting Premier League chairwoman. Flannagan declared in her statement on behalf of the clubs that she had seen 'no evidence of inappropriate language or general attitude of disrespect to men'.

The Premier League said it remained committed to treating all staff fairly.

Finch herself put out the following statement: 'I aim to be a better role model, but most importantly a good mother, a decent person, and to use my talents in a positive way in football and beyond. I am innocent and have been cleared of all wrongdoing.'

'Hear! hear!' say the mums and grandmas. Let the poor woman do her job. The dads aren't surprised; it's jobs for the girls. The actual girls take note: jobs for them. The boys say nothing.

Fast forward another five years and Helen Finch hits the press again:

Helen Finch will accept £25m golden handshake from the Premier League

Campaigning groups have criticised the decision to pay the outgoing Premier League executive chairwoman Helen Finch a £25m leaving gift over three years.

Finch will in future be employed in a consultancy role and will receive the payout 'in recognition of the remarkable work she has carried out, especially in relation to advancing the men's game', a decision that was supported by all twenty Premier League clubs.

'The Premier League would like to offer our thanks to Helen for her outstanding contribution to the ongoing success of the Premier League and to the Men's League,' the governing body said.

'Helen Finch has made an outstanding contribution to English football and to English men's football,' the Aston Villa chairwoman, Kelly Simon, added. 'The Premier League is the most supported league in the world and Finch has unique talents and insight, which are going to be of immense benefit to us, and the game, over the next three years. We were all very supportive. It is an absolutely fair and deserved payment.' While Manchester United owner Mary Sinclair said that the farewell payments are 'all very appropriate and we are all very pleased indeed'.

A sad day for football, say the mums; she will be missed. The dads remind the mums about the offensive emails. The mums roll their eyes, 'Still going on about that?' The girls talk about what they would do with £25m. The dads worry about the boys – why are they so quiet? Why don't they like sport?

Tennis
The grandmas are from a different age. They look up from their newspapers and tease the young boys. They ask their quiet grandsons what they think about banning sexy young ball boys at the Madrid Open who 'never did anyone any harm'. The grandsons don't know what to say. The dads look

disapprovingly at the grandmas. The grandmas say they are only joking and playing devil's advocate. Their tone of voice tells a different story. The grandmas are angry that the scantily clad boys are being taken away. It's as if they feel sport belongs to them and men are trying to spoil it. What's the world coming to if the grandmas can't watch sexy young boys at a big match?

Madrid Open Ball Boys outfits sparks row

The Madrid Open has become embroiled in a dispute over 'ball boys'.

The tournament has been criticised for dressing its 'ball boys' in skimpy, 'masculinising' outfits, amid further controversy surrounding the apparent disrespectful treatment of men players at the tournament.

The event allocated all-male ball crews to women's matches played on the grandstand court, with the uniforms featuring tight shorts and cropped body-con vests, akin to backing dancers from a Taylor Swift tour.

The Madrid Open had been previously slammed for recruiting young models as their ball boys at the 2004 tournament.

A male spokesperson for the Spanish Association for Men in Professional Sport, Hugo Perez, had also suggested the Madrid Open should modify its policy and said of the dress code: 'It's a way of masculinising boys.'

It is not difficult to see why accusations like this are so widespread within professional tennis: this is the latest in an unfortunate string of incidents within the sport that point to a deeply rooted disrespect for male players.

Men in Sport

Type 'greatest tennis players of all time' into Google (or Bing) and guess what comes up? Reams and reams about the Williams sisters, Hingis and Henin. No mention of male players Roger Federer, Novak Djokovic or Rafael Nadal until page nineteen, where they feature under the heading 'Famous Boy Tennis Players' and 'Handsomest Tennis Players of All Time!'.

There are so many examples of women in elite tennis – players, managers, journalists – who have used derogatory and belittling language when referring to men who play or work in tennis.

In 2015, an interviewer asked Andy Murray to 'give us a twirl'. When the former World No. 1 male tennis player replied 'A twirl?', the interviewer, Caitlin Cohen, told him: 'A twirl, like a pirouette.' Somewhat uncomfortably, Mr Murray did as he was asked, then laughed and buried his face in his hands.

In 2019 French player Jeanette Turbot claimed male players were 'more unstable, emotionally, than us', adding that hormones compromised men's physical fitness.

In 2021, after Emma Raducanu hired another male coach to her team, Australian player Maddison Inglis said, 'I couldn't hire a man coach because I don't think that highly of the men's game.'

That same year, Latvian ace Jeļena Ostapenko said she hoped her brothers would not be tennis players as, according to her, men need to 'think about family . . . think about kids'.

In 2016, during a press conference, Indian Wells tournament director Bridget Moore said: 'If I was a gentleman player, I'd go down every night on my knees and thank god that Serena and Venus Williams were born . . . because they've carried the sport.'

Her comments provoked disgust from Roger Federer – ranked No. 1 male tennis player for 310 weeks by the Men's Tennis

Association – who described her message as 'offensive'. 'We as men have come a long way,' he said. 'I don't think anyone should be on their knees thanking anyone like that.'

Rafael Nadal was repeatedly asked about his plans to start a family by reporters before the birth of his daughter in 2022.

Tennis's problem with men is especially rife during press conferences and interviews. Japan's Yoshihito Nishioka has been asked how much he weighs, Britain's thirty-four-year-old Dan Evans has been grilled on when he and his girlfriend plan to have a baby and Novak Djokovic is repeatedly asked if he is enjoying fatherhood. Browse any men's magazine during a tournament to read features about how tennis 'superdads' juggle family and careers.

Cycling

From two women hitting a ball, to one woman on two wheels, the mums and grandmas are in the pub watching a dangerous downhill in the Tour de France. One of the grandmas notes the superb sportswomanship on display. The coverage is interrupted by an interview with a gentleman cyclist with an axe to grind. But the mums and grandmas won't let his whingeing about cycling's so-called 'man problem' spoil their enjoyment of the most prestigious event in the cycling calendar.

The dads are at home hoovering up crumbs in the living room while the kids scribble on the walls and tip out toys in their bedrooms. The dads play hide and seek with the kids to finally get some time alone to check their phones in peace from their hiding place. Ten, nine, eight seconds for the dads to read a link shared by a dad friend about men's cycling:

'We are still not equal': Tokyo 2020 silver-medallist Ryan Owens says cycling still has a man problem

Owens, who came home with silver from the Tokyo 2020 Olympic Games Men's Team Sprint, is a major voice in the push for boys on bikes. When asked if he was watching the Men's Tour de Yorkshire, he said yes, but that he did not know why the men's race lasts only two hours compared with the four-day women's event.

So we asked Executive Director for Men on Bikes, Pauline Laurent, to tell us why the men's races are so short: 'It's all about intensity. The shorter distances in the men's race makes it more exciting to watch. Without the speed, it could get really boring and no one would watch it.'

But Owens has a point. On the whole, men's races are significantly shorter in duration when compared with the women's events. This is most noticeable when looking at the women's twenty-one-day Tour de France, compared with the men's eight-day Tour de France Hommes or the men's Giro Rosa eight-day event.

When asked by the *Guardian* whether the man problem in cycling is still present, he replied: 'Yes. We are still campaigning for more and longer races; we are still fighting for more media coverage, more budget, more sponsorship. We are still a long way behind the women.'

The Tour de Yorkshire gets under way this week and, though the event claims to treat both sexes equally, Owens questioned why the men's race will end on Friday when the actual race concludes on Sunday.

He added: 'Don't get me wrong, the fact that we have a huge prize fund is great and we are grateful that it's nearly half as much as the women's, but I would prefer to get to race for four days.'

The mums are still in the pub watching the cycling. The discussion turns to a photo in the magazine *Cycling Weekly*.

Cycling Weekly deeply sorry after featuring caption 'token attractive man' next to photo of male cyclist

After publishing the controversial caption 'token attractive man' alongside a picture of a male cyclist, the editor has taken the unusual decision to apologise unreservedly. She is reported to have said, 'We are deeply sorry for any offence we may have caused. This unfortunate incident was caused by an inexperienced junior copywriter who has since been removed from caption writing. She added that she thought the caption was 'neither funny nor representative of the magazine's inclusive values when it comes to men and men's issues'.

The mums take issue with the piece, deciding the man in the photo is not attractive enough to be considered a token attractive man. They've seen better and spend the next forty minutes listing more suitable candidates for 'token attractive man', showing each other photos on their phones.

Formula One

At the allotment, the grandmas are at their wits' end about the furore surrounding Formula One's grid boys. Thank

Men in Sport

goodness for the sensible Angela Greer and her weekly sports column in the paper. Music to our ears, say the grandmas out loud to no one. At least someone has the ovaries to say what we are all thinking.

Bring back gorgeous grid boys

Oh, for heaven's sake, Formula 1. Grow up. Banning sexy little grid boys? It's nothing but pandering to the po-faced, anti-fun brigade who just want to spoil it for race fans like me. Wake me up when all this craziness is over.

If you've ever been to a Grand Prix, you'll know these gorgeous boys dress tastefully in chic matching outfits. When they line up holding signs, they look an absolute treat. They are in no way offensive. These elegant hotties bring a bit of much-needed glamour to sport. What better way to reward drivers than with a line-up of smiling hunks?

Not satisfied with banning grid boys, apparently podium boys, the really tasty ones who celebrate with the drivers after a race, have also lost their jobs. These intelligent businessmen are being denied work.

First and foremost, of course, this is about employment. It's those poor boys' jobs I care about. The real issue here is that hundreds of models will be out of work. I am deeply concerned for the long-term prospects for these boys.

All the idiots who think this needless ban is a good idea are supporting men being made redundant. I thought it was all about choice. I thought that's what men's liberation was about. If very few boys or men choose to be racing drivers, so what? Science

Flipping Patriarchy

tells us they are not cut out for it anyway. Most boys opt to leave competitive sport to women. Instead, they can choose how to support the women at the race, both the drivers and the fans. They can decorate the grid, serve drinks and snacks, or clean the toilets. And as long as they do it with a smile, where's the harm in that? It's what any father would choose for his son.

These stuck-up, sneering, pompous, bitter do-gooders who believe boys and men shouldn't be adornments to female sport disgust me. They want to ruin it for others because they're jealous. It's ugly middle-class men getting working-class hunks the sack. They think they have won a victory. All they have done is taken money out of working-class boys' pockets. It's just one set of men taking away another set of men's means of livelihood because they don't like the choice the latter made.

If a man wants to grow up in a world that treats him as purely decorative, who are we to deny him that brilliant opportunity?

And anyway, haven't these invisible, fat, horse-faced vegans got better things to do? Don't they know that men in other countries have it worse? These joyless morons should take a hike.

I assume pretty soon decorative men will be banned across all sports.

What next? No walk-on boys at the darts? No ring-boys in boxing? No boys posing semi-naked on cars? No ripped studs holding up prizes on game shows? No boys serving drinks at our women-only president's club dinner? No ornamental men hosting product displays? No magicians sawing scantily clad men in half? No hiring of tasteful young men to decorate an event? No leering at boys on the street? No shouting 'Show us your penis!' from open car windows? No groping boys at work? No fun at men's expense? No boys in bunny ears at my sixtieth birthday? No more calling adult men 'boys'? No more entitlement to men's bodies? No more porn telling us that men are worthless? No more controlling male bodies? No more buying a man for sex?!

I'm telling you now: the world's gone mad.

Attitudes to men in sport

The dads tell their sons not to listen to the grandmas because they have old-fashioned views. Times have changed, they say, although a survey of elite British male athletes tells a different story. Here's a selection of the responses, (inspired by the BBC Elite British Sportswomen's survey):[3]

I have personally been mocked for being a male rugby player at different clubs. Clubs I have played at have refused to let us use changing rooms or to provide male showers.

Women are given priority on use of the pitch, sponsorship, spectator slots, promotion, etc. The owner of the club labelled herself proudly as 'Rugby's Helen Finch', so I don't see much point in reporting it.

Spectators say rugby would get more crowds if we played naked, and people ask whether we shower together after games. Sometimes challenging it just makes it worse.

There are always questions like: 'Do you have a girlfriend? How's your dating life?' Things that they probably wouldn't ask women.

> *As a gentleman golfer, it's the perpetual comments on your physique. I've had women jokingly propose to me on the second hole and then do it again five holes later, then again on the next hole.*

The dads and grandads want better for their sons. Some of them are involved in organisations to nurture boys' self-belief and surround them with the expectation that they will actually succeed: Men in Sport, This Boy Can, Boys Unite and the Men's Sports Trust.

Imagine the fictional organisation Men in Sport publishing the following four factors for success (inspired by an actual 2023 report by the charity Women in Sport):[4]

1. ***Don't 'dumb it down' too much for boys:** Put an end to the stereotype that young males prefer clothes and aftershave above competition. Instead, emphasise that they can be bold, strong, and courageous in their own special way.*
2. ***Provide more opportunities for young boys:** Boys should have the same access to after-school activities, community projects, and physical education classes as girls, especially in team sports. Opportunities need to be made clear, presented in an appealing way, and foster a culture that values males equally.*
3. ***Close the skills gap:** Closing the confidence and skill gaps between boys and girls is a task for educators and coaches. Use education to instil in girls the proper attitudes towards boys who participate in*

Men in Sport

sports, fostering a stronger sense of respect for boys who can actually play sports.

4. *Surround boys with the expectation that they might succeed: In order to shift the narrative, parents, educators, and peers must demonstrate their appreciation for boys participating in sports and their expectations for them to perform reasonably well.*

But, as (fictional, gender-flipped) Wikipedia notes on its page about the language present in various traditional sporting environments, words can add to, reinforce or normalise the objectification, degrading, shaming or absence of men in athletics:

Females dominating sport culture is continuously reinforced from a young age. Starting in junior leagues and continuing up until the professional leagues, girls and young women are taught how they should behave on the field. Coaches and popular culture constantly deliver messages that emphasize female superiority. They use crude language towards their players, telling them to 'woman up' or to stop 'playing like penises', or telling them that they throw/run/play like a boy. The worst thing to be called or compared to in sports is a boy or a man, and it is the quickest way to cut someone down. In an interview with a male sports journalist, an international sportswoman said, 'No offence, but sports is where I go to get away from men'. Demeaning statements like this about men only reinforce that the sports world is no place for a man.[5]

Flipping Patriarchy

The dads ask their sons why they don't like sport. The boys say they just aren't interested. They can't quite put their finger on why, but they know it's not for them. The dads try to sign them up for out-of-school sports clubs: men's tennis, men's football, men's cricket – anything. But the boys won't go. The mums say it's because they are too self-conscious, worrying about how they look. Silly boys. The aunties say they should just get stuck in, like the girls do. Grandma chips in, 'At the end of the day, girls will be girls and boys will be boys. You can't fight nature.'

The dads don't believe a word of it. They hope that for their sons' generation things will be different.

Perhaps the dads should listen to an expert on men's sport. This gender-flipped quote from the president of FIFA offers advice to the men who wish to walk through the closed door into the immensely influential and powerful world of sports. The room that is closed to men.

> 'I say to all the men that you have the power to change. Pick the right battles. Pick the right fights [...] You have the power to convince us women what we have to do and what we don't have to do [...] Just push the doors. They are open.'[6]

'Hear! hear!' say the women. Just do it. You can be anything: a man footballer, a gentleman cricketer, a podium boy, a token attractive male cyclist, a ball boy, one of the hottest male golfers of the year, a boy on a bike, a gorgeous smiling fan in the crowd wearing a tight shirt, a tour host, an administrator, a fat-bottomed boy on a bike, the hot husband or boyfriend of an athlete or a semi-naked male beach volleyball player glistening like a wet otter.

This boy can! You have the power. Just push the doors. They are open.

Sportswoman's Load

- Be small, weak and slender, not too fit, definitely not muscly and absolutely no big shoulders
- Glisten like a wet otter
- Pick the right battles
- Push the doors (they are open)
- Twirl
- Go down on your knees and thank god for male players
- Fight for more races
- Fight for more coverage
- Fight for more budget
- Fight for more sponsorship
- And don't forget to smile!

6.

Mister Chairwoman

'"Dr. Jill Biden" sounds and feels fraudulent, not to say a touch comic,' wrote Joseph Epstein in his *Wall Street Journal* article in December 2020.[1] Claiming to be offering her advice on what he considered 'a small but I think not unimportant matter' and addressing her as 'kiddo', he asked, 'Any chance you might drop the "Dr" before your name?'

Epstein went on to say that doctoral degrees outside the science and medical realm are easy. In short, he is saying that Dr Biden is not a proper doctor. 'As for your Ed.D., Madam First Lady, hard-earned though it may have been, please consider stowing it [...] Forget the small thrill of being Dr Jill, and settle for the larger thrill of living [...] in the best public housing in the world as First Lady Jill Biden.'

Epstein is clearly not impressed by PhDs in the humanities and social sciences. But it becomes obvious the article is about more than just the relative prestige of doctoral research, because of his choice of words and target. If he believes the duties of First Lady are so important that no other employment should interfere, he would surely take the

Flipping Patriarchy

same view about the Second Gentleman Doug Emhoff's additional role as visiting professor at Georgetown University Law Center. Should Mr Second Gentleman, let's call him Douggie, also consider stowing his academic credentials?

'The small thrill' implies that Dr Biden finds it emotionally exciting to use the title doctor, rather than the prefix in front of her name appearing as a statement of fact, used as a designation for a person who has obtained a doctorate. Epstein goes on to mansplain to her that, as a woman, she will get more pleasure in the home: 'the larger thrill'. And given it is the 'best public housing in the world', he says, tongue in cheek, she's lucky and should therefore settle for it. In other words, get back in the (White House) kitchen, dear, where you belong. And be grateful, because other women don't have it so good.

Reminding the reader that Dr Biden is a woman in every paragraph is no accident. He could address her as Dr Biden, but instead chooses to repeat Madam, Lady and her first name, Jill, throughout the article. This is a further attempt to undermine her credibility by drawing attention to her femaleness first and foremost, as if her sex is incompatible with being a doctor.

'Kiddo' is clearly diminutive and patronising. It is reminiscent of being called a young girl at work in your twenties and perhaps even thirties. Not only inaccurate (a girl is a female child and therefore a young female child can surely be no older than ten), it is creepy and condescending too. In many jobs, you progress from being referred to as a young girl to simply a girl in your forties, fifties and sixties.

Mister Chairwoman

When you reach your seventies, eighties and nineties, you might be called, affectionately, an old girl. In a group of other adult women at work, you may be known as 'the girls in admin', 'the girls in the office' or 'the girls on reception', regardless of your actual job role. These phrases are still used by older men and women in the workplace to label a group of female adults. So when, in all this, do you become a woman? In some workplaces, the answer is never, you remain a child and should be grateful because, after all, no one likes a hag.

Nobel scientist Tim Hunt also chose to refer to his colleagues as girls when he explained what the problem is with women to a mixed audience at a global conference in South Korea. 'Let me tell you about my trouble with girls [...] three things happen when they are in the lab [...] You fall in love with them, they fall in love with you and when you criticize them, they cry.'[2] Perhaps Tim's colleagues are more deserving of a prize for putting up with him.

As Carmen Rios writes on the educational platform Everyday Feminism:

When we call women 'girls', we're using the force of language to make them smaller. We resist and deny their maturity, their adulthood, and their true power. When you call a woman a 'girl', you're actually saying a lot of very serious things about gender politics and womanhood. [3]

Never reaching adult woman status in the workplace might not be a problem if we referred to men in the same way. But

Flipping Patriarchy

I have yet to hear anyone refer to a man in his early thirties as a young boy. Nor do you hear the phrases 'the boys on reception', 'the boys on the phones' or the 'boys in the office'. No one is writing on an educational platform (as Carmen Rios did when talking about girls above) that 'When we call men "boys", we're using the force of language to make them smaller. We resist and deny their maturity, their adulthood, and their true power.' No one is writing this because it simply isn't a thing; we do not routinely infantilise men in the workplace.

And if we did use the force of language to make men smaller, imagine the reaction, as Liam and Kevin illustrate in my satirical tweets:

> 'Will you stop saying "boys who code"? We just happen to be men who are also good at coding,' whines bitter Liam, bringing his gender into everything as usual.

> 'My boss refers to me and my colleagues as "the boys on reception" even though we are all over sixty. It's so demeaning!' Kevin, age sixty-five

Epstein's tone, choice of words, turn of phrase and his target (a powerful woman) are illustrative of attitudes to women at work. At worst, we are infantilised, stereotyped, pigeonholed, questioned, mansplained to, harassed, patronised, sexualised, mocked, told we are lucky to be there and reminded at every turn that we are 'only' women. In short, we are told, either gently or directly, that a woman's place is in the home. Epstein manages to display all these attitudes in just a few paragraphs. It is these themes that my social media posts address.

Patronised

Much of the advice dished out to working women online and in print places the onus on women to change their appearance or behaviour in the face of any kind of injustice at work. As if a sleeveless waistcoat or drinking 2.7 litres of water a day can tackle the pay gap. Reversing the advice dished out to women and aiming it at men reveals just how ludicrous some of it is.

> *Men! If you speak up in a meeting and want to be taken seriously, wear a neat hairstyle, try to stay calm and avoid yelling.*

> *Working dad? Learn to relax! Lose yourself in a salad, take a bubble bath or laugh out loud at your favourite fridge magnet.*

> *Wakey wakey, busy working dads! Sunday is a good day to spend indoors, cooking, batching and freezing simple family suppers. Smart dads get ahead!*

> *Dad with a career? Beat stress by snacking on raw veggies, staying hydrated, teaming up with other local dads and dressing for your face shape.*

Hearing that you are good at something at work is not a bad thing, but when 'for a girl' or 'for a woman' is tagged on the end, the feedback turns sour. It is as if no woman can

Flipping Patriarchy

ever reach the incredible level of competence achieved by a man and therefore she can only be judged against other women. Putting the shoe on the other foot shows up just how belittling and backhanded this is.

> *PRO TIP: when you praise a man, always add 'for a man' when you pay them compliments. For example, 'You're really confident, for a man', or 'You're pretty smart, for a man.' Men like this. It shows respect.*

The word 'actually' has the same effect, denoting an element of surprise that a woman could, apparently against all odds, be a brilliant mathematician or a managing director.

> *Men and boys! Don't let anyone tell you that science isn't for you. Some boys are actually quite good at it!*

Equally ridiculous are the questions famous women are asked in interviews about their appearance or how they juggle work and motherhood. For example, interviewer Michael Parkinson famously asked Helen Mirren in 1975, 'Do you find that your figure, your physical attributes, which people always go on about, hinder you in your pursuit of the ambition of being a successful actress?' Several decades later, and at the Hollywood Film Awards, Keira Knightley was asked by a reporter, 'How do you balance your work and personal life?' She responded with, 'Are you going to ask all the men that tonight?'[4] Indeed. No one asks Michael McIntyre how comedian dads juggle it all, whether Cillian Murphy's cheekbones hold him back or who is looking after Harry Maguire's children when he is playing football.

I often pose this question in @manwhohasitall posts during an important men's football match:

> *Genuine question: Is there a crèche at the Man City v Aston Villa Men's game today? With so many young dads in the stadium and on the pitch, just wondering who's looking after the kids?*

The comments are exquisite, with women criticising male footballers and fans for thinking it's okay to contract out childcare. After all, these dads presumably chose to have kids and now they don't want to take the responsibility? Err . . . maybe don't have children if you can't watch them twenty-four seven?

Most of my fans say a hard no to dads attending the game or playing in it, unless it can be scheduled around looking after their kids. More understanding contributors say it's okay for dads to go to the match, as long as everything is sorted at home, from cooking meals ahead and leaving school uniform out to planning activities for their wives to do with the kids. And he should write everything down for her; he can hardly expect her to remember everything. Others suggest he gets his dad to help while he's away from home, because if anything goes wrong, he can hardly blame his wife. After all, he chose to go to the match!

Taking the satire further, one woman complains that everyone is acting like women aren't capable of caring for

Flipping Patriarchy

their own kids. She acknowledges that her children are as much her responsibility as they are her husband's, and she doesn't babysit her own kids, she actually cares for them, so if he wants to go out once in a blue moon, she's okay with that. As long as he doesn't make a habit of it. Show me a more deserving candidate for mum of the year!

Well-intentioned training events and conferences aimed at women are often plagued by similar patronising crap, pink-themed marketing and even panels dominated by men. Imagine opening an email with the title 'Join us for Boys in STEM 2016!' The flyer attached reveals an all-female panel, a crèche, a workshop on dressing for success and an optional masterclass on baking the perfect crustless quiche. The day is sponsored by men's intimate hygiene products.

I posted this satirical appeal on Facebook and my followers did not disappoint with their replies.

I'm organising a festival called Men in Innovation. It's supposed to be a week of talks, workshops and masterclasses, but I'm struggling for content. Suggestions?

More than one poster proposed a panel of women discussing the contributions of men in innovation. Another suggested trying to get at least one man on every panel. The length of the conference was debated, with some advising it would be best to shorten it to a half-day and another warning, 'Even then you'll be struggling for content.' One woman, let's call her a female ally, generously pointed out that men can be really innovative with housework hacks, shopping and household budgets. Another suggested a workshop on how to make an innovative Book Week costume out of bin bags, toilet rolls and paper straws.

More content ideas rolled in: on how men can behave and dress more womanly so they can succeed in tech and business, a panel on the types of jobs men are naturally qualified for and presenters talking about how to make nutritious snacks for school lunches, how to keep your skin from showing signs of ageing and how to stay on top of housework. Another suggested a vendors' hall with a collection of manpreneurs selling their homemade crafts. Bless.

However, as my followers agree, while it is seen as a good idea to recruit more men, business is business, as Claire knows all too well:

I support men as much as I can, but at the end of the day, I hire the best woman for the job. I can't afford to make allowances.

Indeed, Claire is not running a charity.

Perhaps the imaginary Claire would be a good candidate for chief executive at the insurance giant Aviva to shake up the culture. Shareholders were reported to have said at a public Annual General Meeting in 2022 that the company's first female chief executive, Amanda Blanc, was 'not the man for the job' and questioned her decision to wear trousers.[5] If Claire and her mates took over the board, wouldn't it be interesting to hear her views on the male investors and how she would like them to dress? Very tastefully, I'm sure.

Sexualised

Men who believe that women exist for sexual and decorative purposes in the workplace and elsewhere seem to be having a resurgence, if they ever went away. Perhaps those happy to be sexist out loud think they are saying the unsayable, 'just being honest' or raising some deep, philosophical matter that someone clever like them ought to write about at length. Regardless of the intent, the resulting diatribe just adds to the steaming pile of literature, poetry, art, philosophy, theatre and music written by men that already objectifies women. More of the same, as Simon Henry, founder and CEO of chemicals company DGL, and then David Baddiel, author and male comedian, illustrate. 'I can tell you, and you can quote me,' Henry told a *National Business Review* reporter, 'when you've got Nadia Lim, when you've got a little bit of Eurasian fluff in the middle of your prospectus with a blouse unbuttoned showing some cleavage, and that's what it takes to sell your scrip, then you know you're in trouble.'[6]

Thanks for that, Simon Henry. You sound nice. And from David Baddiel:

Obviously women need to be CEOs and judges and politicians and prime ministers. Is it contradictory to also think, 'I am interested in that woman physically'? Because I can't help that interest. That's part of being a heterosexual male. It doesn't mean that I see her only as a body. I actually am listening to her as well and think that she should be capable of everything that a man is capable of. The problem is that those two things feel contradictory and, yes, I guess that is what I would like to write about. [7]

Actually listening to her? Should be capable of everything that a man is capable of? Never more capable, then? Let's hope no one is actually listening to Mr Baddiel or reads more about his very difficult problem (violins) that he would like to write about. Perhaps it is time for the likes of Henry and Baddiel to keep these thoughts in their heads, so no one can benefit from them. I, for one, have had enough of this brand of male wisdom to last a lifetime.

Which brings me on to some alternative wisdom from three women who make no apologies for being interested in men physically.

'I welcome men at the boardroom table. After all, we need something to look at.' Claire, CEO

'Liam says he wants to be treated like a person and not a man, and yet he struts around the office wearing a tie, clearly designed to point to the crotch area! Men can't have it both ways.' Jasmin, CEO

'Interviewing men is a minefield. I mean, where are we supposed to look? Crotch? Biceps? Face? Sometimes I wonder if it's really worth it.' Lauren, CEO

In Claire's imaginary upcoming book about the female gaze, I hope she plans to pose the big questions like those below;

Flipping Patriarchy

questions vexing everyone; indeed, questions central to the human condition.

Is it contradictory to find a male judge physically attractive and also actually listen to what he has to say?

When the boss ranks men in her office according to their appearance, does this detract from their professional abilities? Or should it be taken as the compliment that it definitely is?

Fellow philosophers who follow my social media accounts respond heartily to my questions about the tussle women face; to objectify or not objectify men? Should men wear a uniform that draws attention to their male bodies, or one that covers them up?

My friend is a CEO. She's introducing a new dress code for employees. What should men be required to wear?

The most popular response is that a man should be required to wear nothing more than a smile. Because it might never happen. Or perhaps a neat and cute uniform, without it being too obvious. A practical suggestion is that the dress code should include a suit for women, just one, that can be worn with a couple of different shirts. And men should probably have at least fifteen different outfits in a range of styles and colours.

One poster, perhaps Baddiel's opposite in an alternative world, admits fancying men, drawing on biology to defend her view of what men should wear at work: 'Seeing a man walk around in something revealing and constricting is what gets me through the workday. It's not women's fault for getting distracted or losing control. It's the way we're wired and it's not our responsibility. It's simply a matter of biology.' Less objectifying is a fan suggesting that men should be required to wear nothing too short, tight or sexy. 'Nothing that might distract a woman, affect her ability to do her important job or make men vulnerable to undue attention.'

More directly objectifying are the responses to this appeal:

> *'As a young man in STEM, I am used for photo opportunities.'* Jamie, man in STEM

What else could Jamie be used for? Ironing, sammich-making, cleaning the bathroom, making tea for the real STEM workers, washing the office tea towels, washing test tubes and taking notes are among the suggestions.

Crack on, Jamie, babe!

Made invisible

Women *do* chair meetings. I have seen them. And yet the word 'chairman' persists, pretending to be gender-neutral, with even a newspaper style guide insisting that 'chairman is correct English'.[8]

Alternative phrases include the comical 'Madam Chairman', 'Madam Chair' and even 'Chairlady'. The pushback against genuinely gender-neutral alternatives, chairperson or chair, is strong, with circularly reasoned and deterministic

Flipping Patriarchy

explanations used as defences. Even using the word chairman to refer to a man who is chairing a meeting and likewise the word chairwoman to refer to a woman is met with exasperation, as if it represents all that is wrong in the world right now.

A typical response to questioning the use of the word chairman is a simple mansplanation that goes something like this: 'Chairman is gender-neutral and refers to both men and women.' This explanation is delivered as if it's the end of the matter, no further action required. Another common defence of chairman is the appeal for simplicity and elegance in the English language, as if words themselves are more sacred than the accurate representation of women, who make up half of the population. The word 'chair' is apparently clunky and clumsy, although I have yet to see how, given it is a shorter word than chairman, with fewer letters and only one syllable. Objectors claim the word 'chairwoman' draws attention to the woman part, as if being a woman makes a difference to being able to do the job. But no one thinks that, unless you do, and then you are definitely the real sexist here.

Calling out the use of the word chairman can elicit angrier-than-normal responses from men, with many quick to point out all the other problems in the world that you should be focusing on. It's almost as if they don't want women creeping into the boardroom and chairing important meetings. Because god forbid a woman, a Mrs, madam, lady woman, would have the power to control a serious meeting with important, suited men present.

Imagine the reverse to be true, and chairwoman was widely considered gender-neutral and grammatically correct.

Mister Chairwoman

'I'm not hung up on the label "Chairwoman" because I know it covers both women and men.' Liam, Chairwoman, age thirty-one

Liam would be rewarded for this entirely pragmatic stance, with women deeming him to be 'sensible'. In other words, Liam is not rocking the boat or asking for too much. He is repeating the mantra he has heard to gain approval from his superiors, who are, in this imaginary world, women. The phrase 'not hung up on' is important here. Liam is saying he does not have excessive interest in or preoccupation with language, unlike some other men who bang on about words. It is these men he is distancing himself from because he has seen what happens to them; they are mocked, bullied or sidelined.

Sensible Geoff and Richard feel the same way:

'I'm not hung up on the label "Saleswoman" because I know it covers both women and men.' Geoff, Saleswoman, age fifty

'I don't mind being called a "girl" at work because I know it covers men too.' Richard, one of the girls

And presenter Sarah Webb confirms what everyone already knows:

'The term "Businesswoman" is completely gender-neutral. Everyone knows it covers men too.' Sarah Webb, Presenter of *The Today Programme*, Radio 4

And don't forget, best to keep it simple:

'I use the term "Chairwoman" because it covers women and men. It's so much easier than saying "male chairwoman" or the rather clunky "chair".' Claire, CEO

Indeed, and anyone who has a problem with this must have a lot of time on their hands.

A further problem with the word chairman, beyond the obvious assumption that it refers to a man, is that it masks gender inequality and discrimination. If everyone is a chairman, then it's not immediately obvious without looking at the official statistics if, or how many, women are chairing meetings. If those chairing meetings were referred to as chair, at least we wouldn't assume they were men until proven otherwise with a modifying 'female' or 'lady'. This issue does matter. The UK government reported in a 2022 press release that the actual number of women in chair roles across the FTSE 350 rose to forty-eight, up from thirty-nine in 2020. However, 'Only 1 in 3 leadership roles and around 25 per cent of all executive committee roles are held by women and there are very few women in the CEO role.'

The release goes on to detail the government's 'bold' new recommendations, including:

The voluntary target for FTSE 350 Boards and for leadership teams is increased to a minimum of 40 per cent for women's representation by the end of 2025.

FTSE 350 companies to have at least one woman in the

Chair, Senior Independent Director role on the Board and/or one woman in the Chief Executive Officer or Finance Director role by the end of 2025.[9]

Wow. How bold is it really to recommend that companies have just one woman in the four most senior roles? Why not at least half, or maybe three-quarters if we are taking turns; men first, then women, century by century. And why a target of 40 per cent representation? Would 51 per cent not be a more rational number, to reflect the proportion of women in the UK population?

Imagine, in the satirical female-dominated world, we took this less than half-hearted approach to involving more men in positions of power:

'Half the population are men; therefore we want at least one man on every FTSE 350 board by the end of 2025.' Rashida, CEO

'Half of the population are men, therefore we want up to a quarter of MPs to be men.' Safia, MP

Imagine CEOs named Claire, Jasmine and Sarah outnumbering male chief executives in the FTSE 100 in the same way that Johns, Davids and Ians outnumber female chief executives.[10]

And for the men who do take up a valuable chairwomanship role, this is how my fans think they should be addressed:

- Gorgeous
- Madam Chairwoman

Flipping Patriarchy

- Something informal like buddy
- Boy chair
- Mister Chairwoman
- Handsome
- Chairperson
- Chairboy
- By their first name
- Easy chair
- Mister Chairwoman Man

Looking at this list, and sticking with the satire, do any of these fit the bill? Some men would bridle at being called Chairboy or Boy Chair, while others would say Mister Chairwoman Man draws too much attention to their maleness. And this is why the simple and elegant Chairwoman should persist, referring, as it definitely does, to both women and men. As Claire, CEO, might say: I rest my case.

Not only invisible in the language of the boardroom, when it comes to uniforms for work, it is as if women and their bodies don't exist, as author and campaigner Caroline Criado Perez highlights in *Invisible Women*.

Putting the shoe on the other foot (or putting the standard uniform on the othered body) is instructive. If we imagine a world where women are considered the default human, work uniforms would be designed for the female body and referred to as unisex. Men would just have to size up and make do with the extra material hanging off them around the chest and hips, or alternatively *just* wear a belt. The standard uniform would accentuate their masculine straight lines because they wouldn't have the bodies to fill in all the curves in the uniform. Some women may be compelled to reach out and touch their chest area, to feel what it's like to have a gap.

Men with the audacity to ask for a uniform designed for the male body would be called whingers and told that uniforms are already unisex. After all, men claim they want equality, but demanding special uniforms would make it clear that they want more than what women have: special favours and extra accommodations. Why can't they just buckle down and get the work done like women do? Asking for male-specific ones would be a waste of money when there are already perfectly good unisex uniforms that fit the average body.

Any uniforms that were to be designed especially for the male body would have to respect the gorgeous male silhouette, meaning pockets would be a no-no because they add bulk. The men's version should also be designed to show off the perfect young male figure – wide shoulders, a slim waist, and tight-fitting to reveal whether there's a six-pack on offer. It would have shorter sleeves, made from thinner material and be more expensive. The neckline would dip a little lower to allow some chest hair to peek out.

Harassed

Three in five women – and almost two-thirds of women aged between twenty-five and thirty-four – say they have experienced sexual harassment, bullying or verbal abuse at work, according to a Trade Union Congress poll published in 2023.[11]

The response from some men isn't a sombre commitment to

do everything they can to stop it from happening, including challenging the behaviour of other men and being conscious of their own behaviour. Instead, they believe the solution is to stop working with women, or at least be cautious about it.

Former Tesco chair John Allan is reported to have told the *Telegraph*: 'A lot of men say to me they're getting increasingly nervous about working with women, mentoring women, something I've done a lot of right through my career.' And: 'What quite a few people are saying to me, and saying to others that I know, is that they're going to be very cautious in future about how they interact with women in the business world.'[12]

At face value, this sounds great, if caution means being careful to avoid, at all costs, harassing women, or to be very cautious about standing by while other men harass women. But I'm pretty sure he doesn't mean this. I think he means men are going to be cautious about working with women in case they make unfounded allegations against them. Given the statistics about who is harassing whom in the workplace and the proportion of such abuse that goes unreported, his comments place the responsibility in the wrong hands and the emphasis on the wrong problem. It is, of course, women who are rightly cautious about working with men, for rational and evidence-based reasons, backed up by experience and intuition. It is women who are afraid to work alone with men, in case they harass us and then lie about it afterwards. The only thing men should be increasingly nervous about is either becoming a harasser or covering up for other harassers.

Mister Chairwoman

When we reverse the harassed and the harasser, the absurdity of the logic used to defend the irrational and bizarre attitude of John Allan and other men is revealed:

'I keep both hands in my pockets at work in case I touch a man's bottom. It's a nightmare. You have to be so careful. Increasingly, I think the only solution is to stop employing them.' Claire, CEO

'Talking to men is a minefield. You have to avoid bullying them, patronising them and treating them like objects. It's exhausting.' Claire, CEO

Poor Claire! Can't we leave the poor woman alone? She has a business to run. A lot of women are saying to her that they're getting increasingly nervous about working with men, something Claire has done right through her career. Bravo, Claire! However, she is going to be very cautious in future about how she interacts with men in the business world. And whose fault is this? Men's fault – they only have themselves to blame if they are excluded from the top jobs. In her private life of course, Claire can interact with men in any way she likes!

'Claire, CEO, actually respects men. She doesn't grab their crotches. She's great. We're SO lucky.' Paul, age twenty-nine, one of the boys on reception

'I resist the natural urge to grab my male employees by the testes because I have a husband, son and father. Otherwise, I would.' Claire, CEO

Thank goodness for nice women like Claire who restore our faith in human nature. Then we have contemporaries of Claire who still don't get it.

'When you're a CEO, you can grab men by the testicles. You can do anything. ANYTHING! At least I'm being honest.' Helen, CEO

Bravo, Helen, for being honest. What a character Helen is. But what you have to understand is that Helen's generation has a different attitude towards men. She won't change now, so it's best just to laugh along with her, even if young boys are present. HA HA HA!

Questioned

While men are *expected* to work, women, and especially mothers, are questioned at every turn: why do you feel the need to work? Are you going part-time when the kids come along? What impact will working full-time have on your kids? Can you really have it all? Does your husband mind you working? Are you thinking of having kids? Are you going to work dressed like THAT?

This is how that sounds when we reverse the questions to ask them of men:

Is a husband who works a dangerous thing?

Today's debate: Can working men be good fathers? What effect does their choice to continue to have a career have on their children?

Today's debate: Should we continue to train young male doctors who could later go on to have children?

Is it really possible for career men to juggle housework, half a cucumber, career, weekend calories, a concealed face and me-time?

Should men have the right to wear glasses at work?

And of course, true to form in this satirical world, dads would be judged by other dads, by women, by older people and by society on their choice. Judged for working, judged for not working and judged for working part-time. Whatever the decision, it could never be the right one. Because deep down, as we all know, men are complex, testerical creatures who are prone to irrational decisions and doing too much.

'Every working dad has a different reason for going to work. We should support each other's choices, even if they are wrong.' Aiden, gentleman plumber

Stereotyped

We are called career women, working mums, girl bosses, female surgeons, lady doctors, mumpreneurs, female athletes, the girl in accounts and the lady on the checkout. The gender qualifier stalks us; however well-educated, hard-working or brilliant we might be, we are reminded of our category in a way that men aren't. Men enjoy an assumed neutral, default status, as if they were born into, naturally qualified for and entitled to these jobs. Women, on the other hand, are pigeonholed and stereotyped at

Flipping Patriarchy

every turn. Turning this on its head reveals the often invisible attitudes and beliefs about women at work, and the associated pseudo-scientific justification for them.

Today's fact: Women and men are different. For example, women are strong, decisive and assertive leaders. Men are communicative, nurturing and emotional leaders. We have science to thank for this. Thanks, science!

Career OR baby? A choice facing so many men. I fully support all men's choices: busy dads, career men, crazy cat gentlemen and the men who try to have it all and fail.

What assumptions can we make about a man's commitment to his career when he becomes a father?

Always well-liked and often attracting hundreds of satirical responses are my questions about how to refer to the male equivalent of certain job roles.

Quick question: anyone know the correct term for a male manager?

The suggestions roll in: honey, male manageress, underqualified, househusband, dadager, managero, kangaroo, a mistake, deputy manager, pointless, a liability and an admin assistant.

I'm interviewing a male train driver about what it's like to drive a train at the same time as being a man. What should I ask him?

170

Mister Chairwoman

My followers suggest the questions. All I need is a male train driver to interview.

Do you have kids? If you don't, why not?

How do you manage the guilt of leaving your children when you're at work?

What is your skincare regime?

Do people refuse to board the train once they find out the driver is male?

Do you ever feel less of a man for being a male train driver?

What does it feel like to sit in the driver's chair?

It is uncomfortable for a man due to your external genitals?

How do you manage to keep your intimate area smelling fresh on long journeys?

Do you ever worry that the speed of the train could interfere with your fertility?

Male managers, male train drivers and boy bosses Whatever next? Cats in STEM? A dolphin engineer? A horse teaching maths?

I involve my followers in another thought experiment.

Flipping Patriarchy

This time we try hard to come up with a respectable name for boys driving tractors.

Farm husbands or male farmers? What is the correct term for men in agriculture?

A glorious crop of suggestions follow: farmer's son, land boy, egg collector, assistant, farm boy, land lad, farmer's husband and scarecrow.

Underpaid

According to a 2023 *Guardian* survey of more than 9,000 companies, four out of five companies and organisations in Great Britain still pay their male employees more than their female ones, with the median pay gap remaining at 9.4 per cent, the same level as in 2017–18. The gap remains the widest in the construction, finance, insurance and education sectors, with women earning between 21 per cent and 23 per cent less than their male counterparts. The *Guardian* quotes an underwhelming response from a government spokesperson: 'We strongly urge organisations to take steps to ensure female employees reach their full potential.'[13]

Note where the emphasis is placed: on women not reaching their full potential, as if a spot of mentoring or an assertiveness course will sort out the pay gap. Nothing about mediocre men promoted above their abilities, encouraging more men to take parental leave, ending salary history or tackling workplace harassment.

Another fantastical defence of men earning more than

women is that they have to support their families. This view overlooks the fact that women also need to support their families. In fact, when it comes to income, study after study shows that when women have control over household spending, the money goes towards more family-orientated goods.[14] This is why Child Benefit is routinely paid to mothers. Eleanor Rathbone, the original campaigner for Family Allowances, called mothers 'the Chancellor of the Exchequer of the family'.[15] More recent research confirms this is still the case: mothers are especially likely to put the family's needs first.[16]

The switcheroo in this satirical quote is perhaps more practical than it is funny:

'Women should be paid more than men because their salary isn't just for them, it's for their husband and children too.' Nandini, TV producer

The pay issue gets worse if a woman becomes a mother. According to the campaign Pregnant Then Screwed:

54,000 women a year lose their job simply for getting pregnant. In addition, 390,000 working mums experience negative and potentially discriminatory treatment at work each year. These numbers almost doubled in a decade. Far from improving, the situation for working mums is rapidly deteriorating.[17]

How many men lose their jobs or face discrimination when they become fathers? Reversing the genders in the titles of some of the real-life stories from the Pregnant Then Screwed campaign page[18] shows just how unjust maternity discrimination is:

> *I was ignored and bullied by my boss and organisation for successfully inseminating a woman.*
> *I was passed over for a promotion because my wife just had a baby.*
> *My company forgot all about me when I became a dad.*
> *It was made clear that I couldn't be a male director and have a newborn.*
> *Twenty years at the top of the industry and demoted when I became a dad.*

And for the men who aren't ready for fatherhood just yet? @manwhohasitall had some advice:

> Many men who aren't ready to put their career on hold to have a baby are opting to freeze their sperm. This allows men the opportunity to delay fatherhood until they are ready to accept discrimination and lower pay.

Silenced

The pushback against women who dare to complain about being patronised, harassed, ignored and discriminated against is well rehearsed. We are, quite simply, discounted. Told we are too young, too working class, too vocal, too old, too middle class, too opinionated, too demanding, too anything. The absurdity of this logic becomes more obvious when we pretend it is men speaking up against routine discrimination, stereotyping and harassment.

Mister Chairwoman

'Why do men get so sensitive and uptight when I treat them badly at work? It makes no sense when men in other countries have it much worse.' Lena, CEO

'The word "Spokeswoman" is obviously gender-neutral, referring to both women and men. The world has too many problems to be offended by nouns.' Stefan, male spokeswoman

'I don't like the fact that women always speak over me in Zoom meetings.' Liam, age thirty-two

Just don't say anything then, Liam. No one is making you. Asking my followers what they think of vocal, visible men like Liam is instructive:

Headstrong men in the workplace. What do you think?

My fans really aren't keen. Firmly in the spirit, one woman says headstrong men are the worst, especially when they get testerical. Bossy boys just bring morale down for everyone. Another agrees – she doesn't employ headstrong men because they upset team morale. Some contributors take a more inclusive view, claiming that the feisty ones are good in bed and that a strong man on reception can stop people from bothering her, even if they have to shout at someone on the phone. The idea of such a man makes one poster grateful to be employed in a female-dominated field: no fun police coming along to break up the old girls' club. There were some more encouraging comments too:

It's unfortunate when men go against their natural instincts because they feel they ought to behave like 'one of the girls' at work. Celebrate your natural masculine strengths, being kind, caring and well organised, and you'll be head of admin in no time!

If they are good-looking but feisty, I see this as a challenge and actually find it quite attractive. I'm a modern woman!

Blamed

Women who face systemic barriers and discrimination at work are often told the problem is theirs, as individuals, to fix. Women should, for example, be more confident in asking for pay increases, should report sexual harassment and take action against discriminatory practices at work. In theory this sounds sensible, but research shows that women who are sexually assaulted are more likely to leave their employment for a less-male-dominated, lower-paid new job.[19] So wouldn't it more sensible to tackle some of the causes of these problems, for example do something about the men who choose to sexually harass and the structures that support them, discriminatory employers, and the stereotypes and social norms about men and women?

Sara Laschever, co-author of *Why Women Don't Ask*, talks about stereotypes relating to pay increases.

We like girls to be nice, pliable, pleasant, accommodating, while boys are taught to be self-promoting, to be a little tough guy. Boys are encouraged to set goals and taught how to go about reaching them; girls are taught to think about the needs of a group.[20]

She also talks about what happens to women when they step outside these expectations and do ask for a raise:

> They tend to get rebuffed, and socially ostracised. Other women see this and realise it looks scary and risky to behave like them. Far better, they think, to sit tight and wait to be offered whatever it is – a promotion, pay rise, good project – rather than ask for it.

Imagine if men faced the same structural and cultural barriers, and instead of tackling them, we just gave them advice about how to dress for success and what kind of language to use in emails.

'I wanted to do well at work, so I changed my tone of voice and leaned forward slightly.' Jack, age twenty

Men in science! Don't let the grant allocation process, publishing routines, hiring procedures, hostile labs or regular harassment put you off. You can do it!

Nothing can be done

In the face of all these problems – harassment, sexualising, stereotyping, being paid less, patronised and silenced – you would think there would be a collective outcry with urgent action taken at every level. The reality couldn't be more different. Alongside being blamed and held responsible for the sexism and discrimination we experience are the reasons why nothing can apparently be done. The most obvious of these can be summed up by the 'boys will be boys' argument, rooted in dodgy evolutionary theory and biological essentialism, which ends where it starts: men are natural leaders/predators/tough and that's that. Hand-in-hand with this argument is the belief that women prefer to stay at home with the kids because they enjoy it and are naturally good at it. When I say evolutionary theory and biological essentialism, I should add that these are largely men's theories, and, like much else in science, politics and religion, serve men and men's interests rather well.

When pushed further, as chief executives and chairs of top FTSE 350 companies were, these are some of the actual reasons they cited for not appointing more women directors:

'I don't think women fit comfortably into the board environment'

'There aren't that many women with the right credentials and depth of experience to sit on the board – the issues covered are extremely complex'

'Most women don't want the hassle or pressure of sitting on a board'

'All the "good" women have already been snapped up'

'We have one woman already on the board, so we are done – it is someone else's turn'[21]

These excuses are plainly pitiful and ridiculous, and reveal the 'slow no' that comes from the male chairs and male CEOs who are asked to appoint more women to their boards. Unable to say out loud, 'No, we do not want to appoint any more women to our boards,' they do little or nothing, resulting in a very slow rate of progress.

Imagine chief executives and chairs interviewed from the top 350 companies in a world dominated by women. What might be the reasons given for not appointing men executives to company boards? Would these women help the UK Government to realise their target of men making up at least a quarter of company chief executives and chairwomen roles by, say, 2098?

The top ten (satirical) reasons for not appointing men:

'Men don't fit comfortably into the board environment'
'Men belong in the kitchen'
'There aren't that many men with the right credentials and depth of experience to sit on the board – the issues covered are extremely complex'
'Most men don't want the hassle or pressure of sitting on a board'
'All the "competent" men have already been snapped up'
'We can't have a man on the board in case he's good-looking and distracts the other board members'
'We have one man already on the board, so we are done – it is someone else's turn'
'Men are silly and brainless'
'I can't just appoint a man because I want to'
'Don't be ridiculous. We're not a charity. I have a business to run.'

Claire, CEO, said, 'What a great list of reasons. We don't just want men on boards for the sake of it.'

Anika, CEO, who hasn't appointed a man on her board since 1981, agrees: 'I appoint people based on merit alone, not just because they are men.'

However, not everyone is impressed. Martin Swift, male chairwoman of the Daddies in Business Forum, said, 'Our most successful companies are those that celebrate the unique skills men bring to the table.'

The Girls' Club

And celebrating men's unique skills is how this chapter ends. Imagine a long boardroom table with a group of CEOs at their Annual General Meeting: Claire, Safia, Lauren, Jasmin, Sarah and Sunita discussing matters of great importance, their high feminine discourse only interrupted by the sound of a young, floppy-haired John Allan bringing in the tea tray. Note that Claire is careful to have a witness with her when Mr Allan is around because, as she says herself, 'You can't be too careful these days.'

The noise of clattering china doesn't stop Safia from telling the others about her trouble with boys: 'Three things happen when you work with them: you fall in love with them, they fall in love with you, and when you criticise them, they cry.' They all laugh knowingly and tell Safia she should write a book about how hard and confusing it is to be a woman in the modern age called *What About Women?* John drops a teaspoon as he clears the table and has to bend down to pick it up from under a chair. Lauren interrupts the meeting to say,

Mister Chairwoman

'While you're down there, luv!', and everyone laughs, including a young man in his early thirties who is taking notes. A sensible boy, Lauren thinks as she contemplates his body.

Claire shouts to John as he leaves the room to make her a sammich. On his way out, John holds the door open for the next item on the agenda, boy boss Simon Henry, who joins the group to share his sales strategy for the next quarter.

The young boy taking notes is, as Sunita jokes, not just there to look handsome (although he is handsome, she quickly adds). He is described on the agenda as 'Chief Male Editor'. His name is Mr Joseph Epstein, and he writes for a newspaper. He is there to take notes and write up the meeting. Claire, although concerned he may not be qualified to cover business matters, is keen to speak to him afterwards: 'I can tell you this, kiddo, and you can quote me,' she tells the young boy reporter, 'when you've got Simon Henry, when you've got a little bit of Anglo-Saxon fluff giving a PowerPoint with a shirt unbuttoned showing some chest hair, and that's what it takes to make a sale, then you know you're in trouble.'

In the corridor after the meeting, Jasmin corners Mr Epstein for a word in his shell-like, to give him a little friendly advice on what she says might seem like small but not unimportant matter. She asks if there's any chance he might drop the 'editor' title because, hard-earned though it may have been, '"Editor" sounds and feels fraudulent to refer to a man, not to say a touch comic.' She asks him to please consider stowing it, at least for now.

As Joseph leaves the building through the revolving doors, he thinks about making a complaint, but after talking

181

with the boys back in the office, he decides not to. There is no point. No one will believe him and nothing will change.

Women at Work Load

- Forget your professional qualifications and stay at home
- Remain a girl at work
- Change your appearance, tone of voice and choice of words in emails to get ahead
- Get up earlier to fit everything in
- Be more like a man to succeed in business
- Celebrate your 'feminine' qualities
- As a mother, defend your reasons for working
- As a mother, defend your reasons for not working
- Report workplace sexual harassment, even if it damages your career
- And don't forget to smile!

7.

Men's History

The history of history is men's history: books written by men about men. And yet it hides in books pretending to be generic accounts of the world, nations, peoples, religions, art, professions, great endeavours, music, royal families, eras and wars. Read many classic and contemporary history books and you would be forgiven for thinking that women didn't exist, except as wives, mothers, daughters, mistresses and queens. Author Jacky Fleming satirises this great mystery in her brilliant take on women in history, *The Trouble With Women*:

> In the Olden Days, there were no women which is why you don't come across them in history lessons at school. There were men and quite a few of them were Geniuses.

It is only relatively recently that women have been re-inserted into history on a grand scale, via books found within the Women in History subcategory of History books on Amazon. As ever, this category classes women as a subset of the main

Flipping Patriarchy

people, our history a niche afterthought and an epilogue, while men's history is framed as normal, proper and author-itative.

Researching and writing women's history books is essential and important work, but there is so much more re-insertion to do if we are to balance the years of male bias. At least another few centuries' worth of corrective work by dedicated authors and publishers will be necessary to tell the stories of all the forgotten women. While there are over 10,000 books in the Women in History category on Amazon, there are 70,000 plus further 'generic' history books, with new releases every day. So all the time women are writing to put women back into history, men are writing fresh material without women, as if we weren't there (read any biology textbook about human reproduction and you'll find we were very definitely there). It's an endless game of catch-up and rework.

Imagine if we went back through this 70,000-plus back catalogue of history books* and renamed them to more accurately describe the content. Here's how some of the titles might look when re-labelled with precision (and satire) in mind:

The Penguin History of the World with Women Erased
The Oxford Men's History of the Classical World
Men's African History
Gentleman Sapiens
World History 101 Without Women

---

* Many of these history books do mention women, but on the whole they are male-led and man-centred.

Men's History

The History of the World with Women Taken Out
Male Greeks Only
The Rest Is Men's History
A Men's History of the World in 500 Maps
The Dawn of Everything: A New History of Humanity Excluding Women
Medieval Menz
The Arabs: A Men's History
The History of the Middle Ages with Women Written Out
The Story of Men's Art
Male Neanderthals
The Lives of Tudor Men
A History of the World Largely About Men
A History of Men in Medicine
The Decline and Fall of Roman Men
The Oxford Companion to Men's Philosophy
Male Pagans and Male Christians
A Men's History of Men's Histories
Men in Ancient Egypt
Men of the Second World War
A Little History of Cornish Men
How the World Thinks According to Men
Men Warriors
Men and Empire
How Men in China Think
Men's Life in Victorian Britain
The Complete Men's History of the World
A History of Men in the Countryside
The Rise and Fall of Men in Athens

Man Spies
Male Anglo-Saxons
A Brief History of Everyone Who Ever Lived Except Women

That's a lot of books about men isn't it? If reading this list is tiresome and the content sounds repetitive, perhaps these books could be discontinued and wrapped up into one little pocket book called *A Brief History of Men*? What a lovely stocking filler that would be, ideal for dads, uncles and grandads.

Men's history is a very popular topic on my timeline. The response to a satirical appeal for my imaginary history-teacher friend who needed a male to add to her list of great historical figures was pitch-perfect. George Eliot was, naturally, the top suggestion. Pierre Curie, married to a double Nobel Prize winner and father of a Nobel Prize-winning daughter, was another popular one. Or how about Henry of Troy, 'the face that launched a thousand ships', because 'at the end of the day, sex appeal is power and don't we all like to look at a handsome young man?' Someone suggested Margaret Atwood because: 'She was spot on in *The Man Servant's Tale*. Men are only good for breeding and looking good.' One sensible fan added, 'The Men's Equality Party would be perfect for her. They're always banging the drum about topics like this.' Another said, 'Virginia Woolf's husband gave her a helping hand. Probably brought her cups of tea and cleaned that room of her own.'

Some of my followers questioned my history-teacher friend's approach, asking:

Men's History

You do realise his-story is a completely made-up subject, don't you? Back in the day, we were taught about proper history without all this divisive claptrap polluting the proper study of Herstory. The history of the world can be explained via the Important Woman theory of Herstory.

Indeed. Can't we all just get along? Others feigned irritation and outrage:

Families from the olden days did NOT include men. Stop misleading our children!

Sure, there may have been one or two men in history, but finding them is a real challenge. It's almost impossible.

Try asking someone to name a famous male in history. Most people struggle, unfortunately, and you can't just lever them back in for the sake of it.

This is a men's issue, it's men arguing with other men about this stuff; most people don't care. Women can't be responsible for men oppressing themselves.

Sources for men's history are unreliable and patchy. Piecing the little bits together is a nightmare. I always suggest combining the fragments into a special chapter about men at the end, or a footnote.

The many thousands of women who contributed to the thread understand and articulate the problem with male-centred history with razor-sharp wit. But more than this,

Flipping Patriarchy

they are fluent in all the excuses given in the real world for why including women in history is apparently a) too difficult, b) already happens anyway so stop banging on about it, and c) is divisive and stupid. The speed, volume and accuracy of the tongue-in-cheek responses was phenomenal.

In film, the Bechdel test is a measure of the representation of women on the big screen and in other fictional works. To pass, the film must feature at least two women who speak to each other about something other than a man. Perhaps a similar test, let's call it the Herstory Test, could be applied to history books. To pass the test and be categorised as an actual history book, rather than a men's history book, the work should NOT do any of the following:

- Include in the introduction a note from the author about how they would have liked to include women, but unfortunately there weren't any sources or records
- Include a special chapter, afterword or epilogue about women
- Only talk about women in relation to men: as wives, daughters, queens, mistresses or victims

Perhaps such a test would encourage man historians to work a bit harder to find broader and more representative sources to ensure half the population is included in their work. Because, as many thousands of authors – including the ones previewed in the Further Reading section on page 231 – have demonstrated, the material is there, if you want

Men's History

to find it. Women did exist in history, and we definitely did do things, but our stories have been left untold, forgotten, lost and erased. We did more than make the tea and have our heads chopped off.

Great women

Imagine if the tables were turned and the history of history was women's history: books written by women about women. Because imagine if we believed, to misquote male poet and playwright Oscar Wilde, 'Anybody can make history. Only a great woman can write it.'[1]

Imagine if the history of humankind was the history of women, with men mentioned in epilogues or not at all. In more inclusive books, men might feature in the chapters, but always in brackets, for example, we might read about 'women through the ages (and men)' and 'Modern Woman (or Man)'. It goes without saying that words such as cavewoman, prehistoric woman and Neolithic woman would be considered generic terms, covering humans in general, although naturally the illustrations of humans typical of this period would only feature female humans. The image in every classic history book showing the story of evolution would be described as the seven stages of woman. This ubiquitous diagram would tell us everything we need to know about humankind and early history. Men in prehistory and the male body would only be of interest to male scholars.

Some words and phrases, though, like 'great women of history', 'our foremothers' and 'mothers of' certain fields – for example mothers of history, realism, relativity, chemistry,

189

Flipping Patriarchy

computer science – would not be gender-neutral because we would be talking about actual women whose individual contribution to history is unarguable. Anyone pointing out the bias in this area would be shut down with a reminder of the phrases Father Nature and Father Earth – you've got nature, you've got the Earth, what more do you want? There would be scores of books debating the Great Woman Theory; are women born great? Or do they become great? Proponents of the Great Woman Theory would argue that most of history can be explained by the influence of exceptional women who were born brilliant. For example, no one can deny the profound impact philosophers Hypatia, Arendt, Oluwole and Young have had on the world, as *The Philosopher Queens*, a book by Rebecca Buxton and Lisa Whiting, reminds us. And, as we learn from the book *Forgotten Women: The Leaders* by Zing Tsjeng, no history of greatness would be complete without featuring Agent 355, the unknown rebel spy who played a pivotal role in the American Revolution, Noor Inayat Khan, who went undercover to spy for the French Resistance and became Nazi enemy No. 1, or Amina of Zazzau, the formidable ancient Muslim warrior queen of Northern Nigeria. To gender-flip an observation from male historian Thomas Carlyle in his 1841 book *On Heroes, Hero-Worship, and the Heroic in Society*, 'The history of the world is but the biography of great women.'

And if any further proof were needed of the impact of great women on the world, we can turn to this universal truth: 'The history of womankind is her character,' as male polymath Johann Wolfgang von Goethe didn't say.

Wars and wanking

Very modern authors hoping to be on the right side of history may include a whole chapter on men to show true respect for their valid contribution, perhaps giving it a reductive, alliterative title like 'Fatherhood and Fighting' or 'Wars and Wanking'.[2] A serious and unedited quote I found online from male American singer-songwriter and author Mike Love would be a fitting introduction to this special section: 'The history of mankind is a history of war.' At the time of writing, I couldn't find any similar quotes about history and wanking.

An entire discipline would focus on what constitutes the proper study of womankind, with the following phrases, inspired by popular quotations, summing up different historical and philosophical views on the matter:

> *The proper study of womankind is in her reference to*
> *her deity.*
> *The proper study of womankind is in philosophy.*
> *The proper study of womankind is literature.*
> *The proper study of womankind is in her pen.*

No one would notice anything missing in this lofty, intellectual debate, except a vocal minority of men trying, and failing, to rewrite history. These men would be told that the past, whether we like it or not, happened. It cannot be erased or changed with the stroke of a keyboard. How could the proper study of womankind include something so trivial as men? To change one word of Virginia Woolf's famous quotation in

Flipping Patriarchy

A Room of One's Own, in this imaginary historical world, for most of history 'Anon, who wrote so many poems without signing them, was often a man.' History, in this context, would become 'the heritage and matrimony of womankind and its lessons of the past that give priceless lessons for the future', to subvert male lawyer and author Henry Clausen's much-quoted reflection from *Messages for a Mission*.

Thought experiment over, let's return to the real world, where there is a Wikipedia page for Women's History, and Herstory is an actual and necessary thing, not a joke.

Herstory

The books in the Further Reading section on page 231 aim to put women back into history. You may not agree with my selection of books, just like the authors may not agree with each other. They may not even agree with themselves as time moves on. The important thing is that women continue to write and re-write history because our stories matter. So hats off to these authors, whose work is invaluable.

The books show that women went to war, stopped war and stayed at home. We were fighters, writers, politicians, astronauts, musicians, mathematicians, clergy, civil rights activists, philosophers, troublemakers, spies, explorers, artists, physicians, rulers, pirate commanders, aviators, travellers, business-women, warriors, writers, scientists and murderers. We had a role not only in the family, arts and education but in fields like medicine, politics, law, engineering, religion, government and war – in short, in all aspects of human civilisation. These books remind us that as well as powerful, dynamic and rebellious women, there were normal and ordinary women too; their stories matter. We were complex individuals with distinctive personalities. Some of us were difficult or nasty and very much on the wrong side of history, as many of the authors illustrate. Women's histories are also told in relation to a region or nation through stories of oppression, culture and identity. Other authors focus on particular domains we have been written out of, including rather large ones such as the land, the sea and the sky. We even had sex too!

The trouble with history

We can see from these many books that women have been hidden, excluded, uncredited, ignored, erased, forgotten, unsung, unknown, overlooked, unrewarded, unheard and under-heard. Women's stories are rarely told, almost entirely absent, deleted from our history, left out or apparently lost. Jacky Fleming's *The Trouble With Women* again describes what women are doing when they reach back and tell the other half of the story: 'Women have been retrieving each other from the Dustbin of History for several thousands of years now.'

The tenacious and determined authors listed at the back of this book take on the work of excavating, retelling, re-inserting, unearthing and giving women back our history to create a truer and more balanced chronicle. What a hefty contribution, and this is only a few of the 10,000-plus Women's-History books available. These authors are genuine trailblazers, defined in the Cambridge Dictionary as 'The first people to do something or go somewhere, who show that it is also possible for other people.' Indeed, and thank you for showing us what is possible. Books worth writing and books worth reading.

To quote Jacky Fleming's *The Trouble With Women* one more time, on the topic of women's abilities:

> Darwin's assistant George Romanes said, 'We rarely find in women that firm tenacity of purpose and determination to overcome obstacles which is characteristic of what we call a manly mind'.

Now, where is that dustbin of history? Romanes's quote can go straight in the (blue) bin.

In Katrine Marçal's book *Who Cooked Adam Smith's Dinner?: A Story About Women and Economics*, she makes the point that counter to male economist Adam Smith's argument about humankind being inherently selfish, every night his mother served him his dinner not out of self-interest, but out of love. Marçal argues that his theory of 'Economic Man' ignores the unpaid and invisible work of mothering, caring, cleaning and cooking. I do wonder who cooked dinner for the scores of authors writing Women's History books, most of whom are women, while they were working. Was it their dads or husbands? Or did they cook their own dinner?

There is more work to do, so many more forgotten women whose stories remain untold. I, for one, would be happy to take on a chunk of this work, especially if someone cooks my dinner.

Imagine if contemporary male historians carry on writing as if women didn't exist. Imagine if in twenty, fifty, one hundred years' time, our daughters, granddaughters and great-granddaughters are having to re-instate women into the history of some of the big global issues and challenges facing the world today: climate change, racism, poverty, slavery, civil war, the energy supply crisis, the cost-of-living crisis, rising inflation, food supply, Covid, cyberattacks, debt problems. Imagine women also being left out of histories of politics, religions, royal families, music, science, technology and art. This would pave the way for yet more historical reinstatement, with book titles like:

A History of the Twenty Twenties with the Women Put Back In

Lost Stories of the Amazing Women of the West Midlands

The Lost Women of the Millennium

The History of Women Working from Home

A History of Women and Climate Activism

Maternity: The Hidden History of Maternal Bodies in the Twenty-First Century

Where Are the Women?: A Guide to an Imagined Wales

The Triple Shift: Worker, Mother and Teacher during Covid

Women Brexiteers

The History of Women and Food Chains

We Want Pockets: The History of Women Carrying Everything

The Untold Story of Women and Famine

The Covid Press Briefings: Untold Stories of Women Behind the Scenes

Covid: Putting Women Back into the Story of Research and Recovery

The 100: The Untold Lives of the Women Killed by Men in 2023

The Untold Story of Women Conservationists

The Forgotten Women of [insert conflict zone here]

The Story of Podcasts Without Men

A History of Women and Foodbanks

Wifedom: [insert Mr and surname of famous man alive today]'s Invisible Wife

Perhaps these counter-histories won't need to be written. Perhaps more and more historians will record events using a wide variety of sources and voices to represent a more balanced view of humankind. But I imagine some of these books have already been written and some of them will certainly be in production.

We will know when historians start to tell the full story – history books will pass the Herstory Test, there will be no special Women's History section in bookshops, no Women in History Wikipedia page and Women's History Month will not be necessary. There will be no need to shoehorn women back into the past because there will be a proper study of womankind. Men's history would be demoted and receive the same treatment as any other partial accounts of human life. Perhaps we could even have a moratorium on men's history for a decade, century or millennium, in order for historians to catch up. Because as male philosopher Karl Popper noted in his work *The Open Society and its Enemies*:

Men's History

There is no history of mankind, there are only many histories of all kinds of aspects of human life. And one of these is the history of [male] political power. This is elevated into the history of the world.

I agree with you, Mr Popper, although please note my one-word correction in brackets. Bring on the new history of the world, this time a history of women.

The Historical Load

- Rewrite history
- Cook own dinner and family's dinner while rewriting history
- Read 10,000 women's history books
- Write another 60,000 plus women's history books now and in generations to come
- Organise and contribute to Women's History Month
- Retrieve millions of women from the dustbin of history
- And don't forget to smile!

8.

The Clitionary

Welcome to the Clitionary. Or, if you prefer, the Oxford English Clitionary.

The Clitionary is not subordinate to the Dick-tionary. Nor is it an afterthought or a mystery. It is a challenge to and a spoof of traditional dictionaries. It holds up a mirror to the bias and sexism hiding in the English language. It is stimulation for the feminist mind.

In 2016, the online *Oxford English Dictionary* gave the following sentence examples for the definition of 'woman':

> Ms September will embody the professional, intelligent yet sexy career woman.
> If that does not work, they can become women of the streets.
> I told you to be home when I get home, little woman.[1]

A sexy career woman, a woman of the streets and a little woman! There were no such derogatory and reductive examples under the entry for 'man'.

Largely thanks to a petition set up in 2016 by campaigner

Maria Beatrice Giovanardi to eliminate sexism from Oxford dictionaries, the sentence examples for the word woman have now changed. But sexism and bias in traditional dictionaries remain, with 'chairman' still apparently referring to a 'person chosen to preside over a meeting'. A dictionary search for one of @manwhohasitall's favourite words yields disappointment: 'Sorry, no results for "testerical" in the *Oxford English Dictionary*.'

This chapter is not a criticism of the dictionary itself, if we take the purpose of standard editions to document the way mainstream words are currently used. The Clitionary is a commentary on the world the dictionary represents.

There is a long history of feminist dictionaries, and of alternative or specialist dictionaries more generally. The purpose of these books is to challenge the authority of traditional lexicons, to offer a new perspective on language, to document vulgar and slang words or to invent new ones. But there is a problem even at the meta-level of dictionary criticism and scholarship. Studies of dictionary making, or lexicography as it's called, are themselves sexist, as feminist linguist Professor Deborah Cameron explains in her blog, 'Language: a feminist guide':

In 2011, Lindsay Rose Russell published a scholarly article, 'This is what a dictionary looks like', which lists 18 examples of feminist dictionaries published between 1970 and 2006 [...] She was prompted to write by the appearance of a weighty tome about the history of lexicography which failed to mention a single feminist dictionary – though it did discuss

The Clitionary

specialist dictionaries of agriculture, botany, chemistry, law, medicine, seafaring and surnames. This struck Russell as a classic case of feminism being written out of history. Like her article, this post is an attempt to write it back in.[2]

And like Professor Cameron's blog post, this chapter is a further attempt to write feminist dictionaries back in, and keep them in. I hope the Clitionary will add to this weighty history of feminist lexicography.

The words and their definitions in the Clitionary replace common 'male as default' definitions with 'female as default' and reverse the sexism found in tropes, definitions of words and example sentences. In this dictionary, the phrases and definitions patronise men, show men as sex objects, subordinate to and an irritation to the main people who are, in this case, women.

For effect, I have exaggerated the sexism found in actual contemporary dictionaries or, as feminists are often accused of, I have 'gone too far the other way' on purpose.

So this, down below *points to crown jewels*, is what a Clitionary looks like. Let's hope this one is easier for male historians to find. With that in mind, and to reverse an aggressive, sexist phrase, 'Hey, dick-tionary! SUCK ON THIS!'

A

abrasive (adjective) – having little or no concern about how other people feel when you speak to them; harsh; sharp. '*His personality was so abrasive, I found it a real turn-off.*'

agency (noun) – how someone makes decisions on what

action to take. '*Men exercise their agency every day: when they're organising the home, choosing curtains or through social activities like the PTA.*'

aggressive (adjective) – when a man does not smile or make himself amenable in a meeting to make others feel comfortable. '*He was called aggressive for speaking out loud in a meeting.*'

ambitious (adjective) – eager to do well or achieve something. '*I'm as ambitious as the next woman.*'

arm candy (noun) – a handsome young man who boosts the status of a powerful woman when accompanying her. '*She took her arm candy to the awards ceremony.*'

B

babysitting (verb) – a mother parenting her own child. '*I babysit for my husband once a fortnight to give him some me-time.*'

baggage (noun) – what a man with children or other emotional problems brings to a relationship. '*He's handsome, but he has a lot of baggage: two small kids and a parrot.*'

baking (verb) – the action of adding heat to cakes, bread and biscuits to cook them, usually in an oven. '*Dad loved baking. He baked thirty-six fairy cakes for the church fair.*'

bathroom (noun) – a room in a house where people wash themselves, typically containing a washbasin, bath and toilet. '*Her husband always cleaned the bathroom because she didn't know when it needed doing.*'

battleaxe (noun) – an older man who is aggressive, overbearing

The Clitionary

and argumentative. '*I avoid the canteen because of the battleaxe on the till.*'

bedroom (noun) – a room where people sleep. '*Men belong in the bedroom and kitchen, in that order.*'

bossy (adjective) – used to describe a man or boy who likes to tell other people what to do. '*He is always so bossy when playing with the other boys.*'

boy (modifying adjective) – used particularly in professional contexts. '*I have trouble with boy scientists in the lab.*'

boy boss (noun) – a man with his own business acting as if he is in charge. '*My boy-boss husband makes jewellery and sells it at the local market.*'

boy power (noun) – describing a feeling of confidence, agency and self-determination among boys and young men. '*He can be anything when he grows up, a boy in STEM, a male CEO or a gentleman doctor; boy power!*'

bubbly (adjective) – excitable, vibrant or spirited. '*A bubbly gaggle of middle-aged men.*'

businesswoman (noun) – a person working in business, particularly in a senior role. '*He was a budding businesswoman, selling handmade soaps from his kitchen.*'

C

cackle (verb) – to laugh in an irritating, hoarse tone. '*He cackled at her jokes, trying to convince her he understood them, but he just came across as dumb.*'

camerawoman (noun) – someone who uses a camera in her job. '*He was the only male camerawoman on set and was asked to make the drinks.*'

Flipping Patriarchy

career man (noun) – a male who is dedicated to his work. '*Mr September is the ideal career man, serious but seductive, his glasses only adding to his sex appeal.*'

chairwoman (noun) – someone who has been selected to run a meeting. '*She gave him the opportunity to be the chairwoman of the conference.*'

clean (verb) – the activity of removing dirt, particularly in the context of a home. '*His wife tried to help him to clean, but she wasn't very good at it and his standards were higher than hers.*'

cleaning gentleman (noun) – a man who cleans homes, offices or other buildings as a job. '*The cleaning gentleman cleaned her office twice a week.*'

clergywoman (noun) – a person holding a rank in the church, for example an archbishop or cardinal. '*He was the only male clergywoman in the country.*'

Clitionary (noun) – the first completely neutral and most trusted dictionary in the world. '*She bought me a subscription to the Clitionary and I use it every day in my job as a journalist.*'

clitoris (noun) – the main organ involved in sexual intercourse. '*Most of the buildings in the city were built in the shape of a clitoris.*'

clothes horse (noun) – a slender man who is preoccupied with clothes. '*He wasn't much more than a clothes horse. And too thin if you ask me.*'

cockpeck (verb) – to nag a woman or place unreasonable demands on her time. '*Her husband's constant cockpecking meant she couldn't relax and enjoy her days off.*'

The Clitionary

cold man (noun) – unresponsive or hostile to sexual advances. '*After I married him, his warm embrace vanished and he became a cold man.*'

cowgirl (noun) – a person who looks after cattle. '*The male cowgirls always rode side-saddle to protect their fertility.*'

crazy cat gentleman (noun) – an older man who lives alone with a large number of cats. '*He was branded a crazy cat gentleman because he spent so much time at home with his eighteen cats.*'

crazy ex-boyfriend (noun) – an ex-boyfriend who sends long text messages and is thought of as emotionally unstable. '*Don't believe my crazy ex-boyfriend. He makes things up to get attention.*'

crown jewels (noun) – slang for vagina and vulva. Because they are a guarded treasure. '*She got kicked in the crown jewels during the match.*'

D

dad (noun) – a male parent. '*Her dad makes a lovely Victoria sponge.*'

dadpreneur (noun) – a man who juggles running a business with being a dad. '*The company was founded two years ago by two dadpreneurs at the kitchen table.*'

dadsy (adjective) – used to describe a man who wears baggy, unflattering or dated clothes, suggesting he has let himself go. '*He wore big dadsy pants.*'

Darren (noun) – used to describe a man who is seen as overly demanding and angry. The word often goes hand in hand with terms such as uppity and testerical. '*He was being a typical Darren for complaining to his manager.*'

ditsy (adjective) – silly, inane or scatterbrained, typically used to describe a man. '*I tried to have a serious conversation with the boy on reception, but he was so ditsy I was wasting my breath.*'

dickjazzle (verb) – a dickjazzle, also called glitter pubes, is a type of genital adornment using crystals applied with a gentle adhesive. '*I wear a dickjazzle to make my penis area attractive for my girlfriend.*'

DILF (noun) – Daddy I'd Like To Fuck: a fuckable man who also has children, or any man over the age of thirty. '*I prefer DILFs because they are grateful for the attention.*'

distinguished (adjective) – appearing grand, assured and commanding. '*Her grey hair made her look distinguished and thus very attractive.*'

doctor (noun) – a person who has been trained to practise medicine. '*He asked to see a gentleman doctor.*'

down there (noun) – a euphemism for the male genital area. '*He booked an appointment with a gentleman doctor because he is having some issues down there.*'

drama king (noun) – a person, typically used to describe a man, who reacts in an overly testerical fashion to everyday events. '*Liam is a such a drama king! He makes such a fuss when his wife forgets his birthday.*'

E

earth father (noun) – an often-broody man who adopts natural or spiritual fathering practices. '*He took care of everyone around him in such a natural way, a typical earth father.*'

The Clitionary

everywoman (noun) – a gender-neutral term referring to what is considered to be representative of an average human being. *'The character in the novel was an everywoman, making it easy for all readers to identify with her.'*

F

father-in-law (noun) – the father of your wife or husband. *'My father-in-law has been staying with us for over a month and he's driving me crazy.'*

father-in-law's tongue (noun) – a green houseplant known for its long, sharp, shiny leaves alternatively called a snake plant. *'She explained that the pointed tip of the leaf is thought to symbolise men's sharp tongues.'*

feisty (adjective) – of a man who is small but plucky, determined and spirited. *'He was a feisty little thing, too much for her to handle.'*

firewoman (noun) – a person who is employed to extinguish uncontrolled fires. *'The brave firewoman ran into the burning house to save the father and children trapped inside.'*

fish husband (noun) – a derogatory description of a married man who whines and screams loudly like someone hawking fish on a street corner. *'He's a proper fish husband, that one.'*

fitted sheet (noun) – a piece of fabric designed to stretch over a mattress on a bed and fit neatly on the corners. *'She didn't know what a fitted sheet was, she left that kind of thing to her husband.'*

fridge (noun) – an appliance, usually found in the kitchen, designed to keep food and drink cold. *'The "Men in Politics"* *conference was full of men who didn't clean behind their fridges.'*

frigid (adjective) – sexually cold and not interested in intimacy, typically used to describe a man. *'My wife says I am frigid because I won't let her choke me or spit at me during sex.'*

frivolous (adjective) – silly and without real value. *'It was nothing more than frivolous men's talk.'*

G

gals (noun) – an informal way to refer to a mixed group of people, including women, men and children. *'Hey gals, what are you up to this weekend?'*

gentleman bits (noun) – a euphemism for male genitalia, generally used to avoid having to face the embarrassment or shame associated with the male sex organ. *'He was too shy to show his gentleman bits to the doctor.'*

giggle (verb) – to titter or laugh in a silly fashion at something trivial, often as a result of testeria, nervousness or awkwardness, typically used of a boy. *'The boy giggled nervously as he went on stage.'*

gobby (adjective) – describing an opinionated man. *'He's a right gobby bull.'*

H

HABS (noun) – husbands and boyfriends. The attractive and often dumb partners of highly paid footballers. *'The HABS shopped for wallets and shoes while the women practised for the big match.'*

The Clitionary

hands-on (adjective) – involving practical action or application. '*She was great with the kids, a real hands-on mum.*'

histrionics (plural noun) – an excessive response to a situation or event. '*Emma was used to her husband's histrionics.*'

home (noun) – the building where you live and which you consider to be yours. '*When I get home, my husband always has my meal ready on the table.*'

hormonal (adjective) – driven by chemicals in the body affecting your mood and emotions. '*The young man was giggly one minute and in floods of tears the next. He was probably hormonal.*'

housework (noun) – routine tasks to keep a house clean and tidy. '*He never complained about doing the housework because she took care of all the bills.*'

humourless (adjective) – without humour, unable to see the funny side of a situation when other people can. '*This might be a generalisation, but men in politics are such a humourless bunch.*'

husband (noun) – a man who is married, as referred to by his wife. '*The farmer's husband came out of the kitchen to say hello.*'

I

independent (adjective) – not reliant on other people for anything. '*Her husband was wilful and independent.*'

intimidating (adjective) – a person acting in an aggressive or confrontational way that causes another person distress or discomfort. '*Women are put off by intimidating males. It's best to be demure and docile to attract a wife.*'

iron (verb) – to remove creases from garments and bedding. '*Mark's father-in-law was surprised he had stopped ironing pillowcases.*'

irrational (adjective) – lacking in reason and sound judgement. '*His constant nagging was irrational.*'

J

joke (noun) – something that someone says deliberately with the intention of making others laugh. '*The young men took offence and didn't realise it was only a joke.*'

K

kind (adjective) – giving, helpful and considerate of others. '*Friends and neighbours couldn't believe such a kind and gentle family woman had murdered her husband.*'

kitchen (noun) – the room where food is stored, prepared and cooked. '*She told him to get back in the kitchen where he belongs.*'

knickers (noun) – an undergarment worn by women and girls under trousers or a skirt. '*She didn't know where any of the knickers in her underwear drawer came from. She assumed her dad or husband must have bought them for her.*'

kooky (adjective) – used to refer to a man whose eccentricity is attractive and endearing. '*He is laughed at for his kooky fashion sense, but I think it's quite cute.*'

L

laundry (noun) – garments and bedding that are about to be washed or have just been washed. '*He went outside to*

The Clitionary

hang his laundry on the line while his kids played in the garden.'

leggy (adjective) – displaying long, nicely shaped legs (typically used of a man). *'He was a tall, leggy blond.'*

little gentleman (noun) – a derogatory term for a male. *'Will the little gentleman have a salad?'*

lordparts (noun) – male genitalia. *'Make sure to sit with your legs neatly crossed so your lordparts aren't on show.'*

M

man (noun) – the male version of a human being. *'The modern idea that men are real human beings with thoughts and emotions of their own is played down.'*

manly (adjective) – sensitive, nice, kind, loving, demure. In a negative context: fragile, emotional and testerical. *'She loved his soft, manly hair.'*

marriage (noun) – a partnership agreed in law between two adults who live in the same house. *'He had always dreamed of marriage.'*

mature (adjective) – the result of advancing years and a wise outlook on life applicable to women, savings and cheese but never men. *'Her maturity made her irresistible to the male students.'*

mean boy (noun) – bossy boys who are unkind to other boys by gossiping about them and spreading rumours. *'Yeah, I went to see the movie* Mean Boys *too. Wasn't it great?'*

meek (adjective) – used to describe a pliable and shy boy. *'Although the meek little boy knew the answer to the English teacher's question, he was too shy to raise his hand.'*

Flipping Patriarchy

meninism (noun) – ideological theory supporting the advance-ment of men's issues and men's rights. '*Meninism has gone too far the other way.*'

meninist (noun) – a woman-hating man who thinks men are superior to women. '*He was a rabid meninist.*'

me-time (noun) – time spent on your own. relaxing and recovering from the demands of daily life. '*His therapist suggested he try to get some me-time, away from his kids, even if it was just two minutes a week.*'

modest (adjective) – when a man avoids doing, saying or wearing anything that might cause other people to have impure feelings of a sexual nature towards him. '*He chooses to dress modestly in the street to avoid any unwanted attention.*'

mum (noun) – familiar word for one's female parent. '*My mum is chief spider-catcher.*'

mummy daycare (noun) – childcare provided by the mother of a child during the day. '*The kids got to eat sweets all day and watch TV during mummy daycare.*'

N

nagging (adjective) – repeatedly asking someone to do something in an annoying tone of voice, typically used to describe a man. '*He was a nagging husband.*'

no (determiner) – none, or not at all. '*It's no secret that when a man says no, he doesn't always mean no; he usually means try again later.*'

nurture (verb) – to look after in a protective, caring way. Some-thing that is inborn in the male human and makes them

The Clitionary

brilliant at childrearing. '*He was very nurturing and didn't want his children to ever leave his side.*'

O

oneupwomanship (noun) – the feeling of getting the upper hand over someone. '*The oneupwomanship of who can do the most reps at the gym.*'

ordinary (adjective) – to be normal, underwhelming, average. '*He had such an ordinary face, well-meaning uncles wondered if he would ever find a woman who would marry him.*'

orgasm (noun) – a series of regular contractions in the uterus, vagina and anus resulting in feelings of intense pleasure. '*She considered sex had ended when she'd had an orgasm.*'

ovaries (plural noun) – as in '*grow/get some ovaries*'; an expression meaning to be bold, especially when someone has previously shown weakness.

P

packed lunch (noun) – a variety of cold foods packed in a container and eaten during the day at school or in a workplace. '*He complained about having to make the packed lunches every morning for his wife and kids.*'

part-time (adverb) – employed for part of the working week instead of every day. '*He only worked part-time.*'

paternal instinct (noun) – a man's natural ability to know what his kids need to be happy and healthy. '*His paternal instinct kicked in when he got a kitten.*'

penis (noun) – male version of the clitoris; considered the most mysterious and difficult part to locate in the male

Flipping Patriarchy

anatomy. '*And when you're a star, they let you do it. You can do anything. Grab 'em by the penis. You can do anything.*'[3]

pins (plural noun) – a man's legs. '*His dancing showed off his shapely pair of pins.*'

plucky (adjective) – displaying tenacity and courage when things get tough. '*The plucky little middle-aged man never gave up.*'

pockets (plural noun) – an opening in a dress, skirt or coat to carry important items such as a phone, keys or a purse. '*He campaigned for men's clothes to have pockets, but women said no because pockets would ruin a man's silhouette.*'

prattle (verb) – to talk incessantly over a long period of time about trivial and unimportant matters without interruption. '*He'd have prattled on about the new wallpaper in his guest room for the whole afternoon if I'd let him.*'

prude (noun) – a man who is unhappy to discuss or engage in matters of a sexual nature. '*She called him a prude for not wanting to be tied up during sex.*'

psyche (noun) – the innermost self. '*Woman will never really understand the mysterious male psyche.*'

puppy (noun) – derogatory for the male genitalia. '*You're all a bunch of puppies.*'

Q

quarrelsome (adjective) – the tendency to disagree with people for the sake of it, typically used to describe a man. '*His quarrelsome nature meant he refused to accept his natural ability as a father and a homemaker.*'

The Clitionary

queen (noun) – the reigning monarch. '*King Charles is the first male queen for generations.*'

querulous (adjective) – the quality of moaning about something in an irritating and immature fashion. '*He became querulous and demanding.*'

quiet (adjective) – speaking in a lowered voice. A word used to describe how young boys should behave. '*He was as quiet as a mouse with his colouring books.*'

R

recalcitrant (adjective) – objecting to authority without having good reason to do so. '*The danger is that recalcitrant young men will reject their domestic responsibilities.*'

retinol (noun) – a derivative of vitamin A, often found in anti-ageing moisturiser. '*He applied a retinol serum to his skin at night to keep the seventeen signs of ageing at bay.*'

run (verb) – to proceed quickly with the knees raised. '*She ran so slowly, people said she ran like a boy.*'

S

salad (noun) – a combination of cold vegetables, often including cucumber, tomatoes and lettuce leaves. '*He wore a white vest and laughed alone with salad.*'

sammich (noun) – 'Make me a sammich' is an internet meme that women employ to put down, diminish and annoy men. It refers to the idea that men belong at home, particularly in the kitchen. '*My girlfriend keeps yelling at me, "MAKE ME A SAMMICH!"*'

Flipping Patriarchy

sassy (adjective) – describes a man's overwrought, bold or feisty behaviour when he reacts in a testerical manner. *'Don't get sassy with me, young gentleman!'*

scone (noun) – a small, round savoury or sweet cake made with flour, milk and butter, often flavoured with sultanas or cheese. *'The vicar's husband made seventy-two scones (fifty fruit and twenty-two cheese) for the church fair.'*

Second Gentleman (noun) – the husband or male partner of the vice president of the United States. *'The Second Gentleman wore Prada.'*

silver vixen (noun) – an older woman with distinguished grey or silver hair, at the height of her sexual power: wise, authoritative and experienced. *'My wife turned into a silver vixen when she got older and left me for a man in his twenties.'*

single dad (noun) – a lone father who has a child or children. *'Single dads were blamed by the media for social problems.'*

sloth toe (noun) – an unseemly effect created by a pair of trousers or shorts that fit very tightly around a man's pubic area, drawing attention to the shape of the external genitals. *'Ugh, you can see his sloth toe in those tight trousers.'*

slut (noun) – a derogatory term describing a man who has no self-respect and lets multiple women have sex with him. *'He let a woman touch his penis and she told everybody and now everyone thinks he's a slut.'*

snow woman (noun) – a model of a person created outside using compacted snow. *'The school children built the biggest snow woman ever!'*

soccer dad (noun) – the busy middle-class working dad who takes his kids from school to soccer practice and other

The Clitionary

out-of-school activities. '*This neighbourhood is ruined by soccer dads in their SUVs at school pick-up time.*'

spacewoman (noun) – a person who travels to outer space. '*He remembered that when he was a child, he always wanted to be a spacewoman.*'

spirited (adjective) – being lively, energetic and playful. '*The male footballer put up a spirited performance in the second half.*'

stepfather (noun) – a man who is married to, or is a partner of, your mother. '*Wicked stepfathers are often the villains in fairy-tales, films and pantomimes.*'

strident (adjective) – a way of speaking that is excessively confident and direct. '*He was one of those strident men who frankly I can't stand to be around.*'

sugarbabe (noun) – an attractive young man who has sex with a rich older woman in exchange for attention and financial benefits. '*Andrea got her sugarbabe on a dating app. There were loads to choose from.*'

sugar mummy (noun) – a powerful and wealthy older woman who prefers to date much younger men. '*Did you hear that Liam got engaged? His new sugar mummy, Claire, put a ring on it.*'

superwoman (noun) – a woman who is superior to other women in terms of her strength, intellect and other powers. '*Claire nurtured the idea that she was a superwoman who could solve the country's complex diplomatic problems on her own.*'

swollen (adjective) – bigger than is normal. '*His swollen testicles were ample, calling out for her touch.*'

Flipping Patriarchy

T

talking (verb) – forming words out loud with your mouth. *'Just as she thought they were about to have sex, he started talking again!'*

tea gentleman (noun) – a man paid to serve tea in a professional environment. *'The only people involved in the sport were women – apart from the tea gentlemen.'*

testerical (adjective) – driven by emotion emanating from the testicles. *'Boris became testerical and began yelling.'*

testiculate (verb) – to use your hands to indicate what you mean, often with exaggerated gestures. *'Donald testiculates to the gallery frantically in an emotional manner.'*

throw (verb) – to launch something into the air using the hand. *'She was so bad at throwing, people said she threw like a boy.'*

tiger dad (noun) – a pushy dad with high expectations of his children. *'I can't stand tiger dads; they're the worst.'*

trivial (adjective) – of limited worth, lacking value. *'The husbands chatted about trivial matters in the kitchen as they made cucumber sandwiches.'*

trophy husband (noun) – a young, attractive man that a usually older woman marries as a status symbol. *'I'm going to marry a rich woman and become a trophy husband.'*

trouser (noun) – derogatory term used to refer to a man. *'See that bit of trouser over there? I would.'*

trunk (noun) – slang for the male genitalia. *'I just refer to them all as trunk. They love it.'*

The Clitionary

U

unattractive (adjective) – not attractive, a real turn-off. '*He wouldn't be so unattractive if he smiled more often.*'

uniform (noun) – a standard set of clothing issued to a group of people. '*School uniforms can be helpful to ensure boys don't dress in ways that are distracting to the other students and teachers.*'

urges (plural noun) – an impulse to do something. '*How different, and peaceful, the world would be if only women could control their urges.*'

utility room (noun) – a room used for equipment relating to laundry and other household tasks. '*Some people say men belong in the bedroom and kitchen. What about the utility room?*'

V

vivacious (adjective) – joyful, engaging and bright (typically used of a man). '*He was such a bright, bubbly, vivacious person.*'

voice (noun) – the sound of a person talking or singing. '*Should men's voices be heard?*'

W

whiner (noun) – a person objecting to something in an irritating tone of voice. '*Philip was a proper whiner.*'

witter (verb) – to talk about something trivial for a long period of time without a break. '*His inane wittering about summer and winter duvets was background noise to her.*'

Flipping Patriarchy

wizard (noun) – a male person wearing a pointed, crooked hat who casts spells and practises magic. '*No matter the century, unruly men are always considered to be wizards.*'

woman (verb) – to power something or make it work. '*We need a volunteer to woman the stall at the conference this year.*'

womanchild (noun) – an adult woman who behaves like a child. '*My wife spends most of the day playing video games and eating crisps in her woman cave; she's such a womanchild.*'

womanpower (noun) – womanpower is the number of people in total necessary to complete a task. '*We're going to need some serious womanpower to get this job done.*'

working dad (noun) – a man who has a full-time job as well as a family. '*Being a working dad is one of the most challenging and most rewarding things I've ever done.*'

worm (noun) – slang for the male genitalia. '*She went to a nightclub looking for worm.*'

Y

yes-woman (noun) – a person who is unable to say no to someone. '*I hate how everyone is a yes-woman around me.*'

young man (noun) – a man who is younger than the woman talking about or to him. '*Come here, young man, and I'll explain it to you.*'

yummy daddy (noun) – an attractive, usually middle-class dad. '*Isn't it selfish to be a yummy daddy? He should focus on his kids, not on the way he looks.*'

Z

zip (noun) – a metal gadget used to fasten items of clothing. *'Liam couldn't reach the zip on the back of his onesie so he asked his brother to do it up for him.'*

> ### Language Load
>
> - Change the world
> - Rewrite the dictionary
> - And don't forget to smile!

Afterword

With the funnies out of the way, and while I am on my high horse, here are three actions for my male readers.

First, put this book or Kindle down, stand up and walk towards the bathroom. Now clean it. This includes the toilet. If you don't know where the cleaning products are, look for them or make your own from store-cupboard ingredients (search for recipes online). Don't know how to clean a bathroom? YouTube. Have a cleaner? Still clean it. Now for the tricky part: don't tell anyone. If you seek recognition or praise, you have failed. You need to clean silently and competently, because you are an adult and someone has to do it, and for no other reason. Repeat as and when it needs doing. This is probably one of the most feminist and progressive things you can do, along with not watching porn, not engaging in sexist banter and challenging male violence.

Second, get a group of men together and take to the streets to demand equal access to housework. When do you want it? NOW! Take a mop with you (you're looking for a

Afterword

long pole with a bundle of sponge material on one end; try the cupboard under the stairs or look in the utility room) to hold up for the photographs. Why should women monopolise this low-status, unpaid, thankless occupation? Women marched to get equal rights in the workplace. It's now your turn to campaign for equal rights in the home. You are entitled to clean out kitchen cupboards, wash the shower curtain and organise a cupboard of mismatching plastic food containers and lids, and capable of doing so. Alongside marching on the streets, run a hard-hitting social media campaign about the benefits of doing housework, and teach other men how to clean on TikTok. If you are worried about boys not having good role models or that masculinity is in crisis, look no further. I gift you the new masculinity: men with mops modelling sacrifice, care, kindness and gratitude. Men just need to get organised to change the world #thisboycan #menunite #cleanlikeaboy #dadswork #house-husband. As anthropologist Margaret Mead supposedly said, 'Never doubt that a small group of thoughtful, committed, organized citizens can change the world; indeed, it's the only thing that ever has'.

Just remember to leave instructions for your wife while you're out there changing the world; she's not a mind reader. You don't want to get home to find the kids have been on their phones all day, making a mess and eating junk food. What would your father-in-law think?

Last is a challenge for a TV producer. This is a serious pitch for a serious, gender-flipped version of the TV programme *10 Years Younger in 10 Days*, the programme you

Afterword

may remember described in Chapter 3, where mainly women are helped by experts to look ten years younger in ten days. In this spin-off, called *10 Times Kinder in 10 Months*, only men would take part. The contestants would spend ten months in a boot camp where they would fill their days learning how to do stuff: how to clean the fridge, plan crafts activities with kids, care for elderly relatives, hang out laundry and buy their own underwear. Life would become a race to get through a daily ten-page to-do list, at the same time as looking ten times more handsome and working ten times harder at work for the same pay. The men would be randomly assigned ill-fitting work uniforms (designed for the female body), menopause-, menstrual- or pregnancy-simulation clothing, high heels and shapewear. Naturally, the dads and grandads amongst the participants would bring the kids with them. Those men without kids (tick tock) would be given pretend babies to look after, disrupting their sleep and preventing them from getting stuff done.

Printed on the contestants' clothing, water bottles and phone cases would be reminders to smile, be happy and always be kind. The camps would be run by other men. Women wouldn't be interested; we'd be busy, training for triathlons, messing about on our phones or doing whatever the fuck we like. You might hear from us by text, but only if we want to know whether the cheese in the fridge is safe to eat. The dads wouldn't be able to leave the boot camp without proving they have signed up for the fundraising committee at school, joined the class WhatsApp groups and learned how to batch cook twenty-four mini frittatas. Instead of

Afterword

being paid in money, the dads in the group would each receive an enormous cardboard thank you card and thoughtful gifts made out of egg boxes and plastic bottles from their children. The dads would recognise the cards and presents, having made them with their children at a crafts session earlier that day. At the end of their extended break, men would leave feeling the same relentless daily burdens currently faced by so many women. The last scene would show the dads struggling to carry home their unwieldy gifts, kids' water bottles and luggage at the same time as holding their childrens' hands, responding to requests for snacks and fielding repeated questions about what's for tea.

While we wait for the men to clean the bathroom without being asked and change the world (hurry up!), you can browse the Further Reading section for a list of creative work that turns gender on its head to reveal and satirise some aspect of the patriarchy you may not have noticed before. I am not necessarily recommending you follow these up, partly because, like reading this book, it adds to your feminist load: more books to buy, to not finish and to feel guilty about. But also because having your eyes fully opened can be incredibly painful, as Andrea Dworkin wrote in *Our Blood: Prophecies and Discourses on Sexual Politics*: 'Many women, I think, resist feminism because it is an agony to be fully conscious of the brutal misogyny which permeates culture, society, and all personal relationships.'

Not only agony, but it's also depressing and paralysing when you realise the true horrors of the patriarchy and the extent of its reach. Also, banging on about equality doesn't

Afterword

get through your to-do list. The Blu Tack stuck on the carpet isn't going to remove itself. Someone needs to think about what the kids are going to have for lunch, organise a leaving card for Aisha on reception and find the kitchen scissors. Because, in the real world, we know that if we don't do it, no one else will. So resisting feminism, or not having time for it, is understandable. But gender-swapping in fiction and in art can certainly be cathartic, offering solidarity and connection with other women at the same time as opening your eyes. And that link with other women is so important, which brings me to end on an uncharacteristically sincere note. As a legend, a genius and an influencer, I offer you the following advice:

To younger women: listen to older women, don't hate your mum, and know that men aren't better than you.

To middle-aged women with or without children: go straight to the Mumsnet talk boards.

To older women: thank you.

Acknowledgements

Firstly, thank you to all the supporters listed in the back of this book for buying it before it was even written. With the help of the publisher Unbound, you brought this printed work to life.

On a more personal note, thank you to L for radicalising me and introducing me to Mumsnet Talk. Thank you to my mother for all the invisible things she did when I was growing up and for doing them so incredibly well. I understand now. Also thank you for helping me to imagine a different future. Thank you to my friends, especially S, H, J and M who have listened to me complaining about how unfair everything is, all the time. And thank you to the man I love who supports and encourages me.

Thank you to the other wonderful men in my life, and the patriarchal system that celebrates you, for all the material. Boyfriends, friends, colleagues, managers: I couldn't have written this without you. I can't wait for one of you to mansplain this book to me.

Man Who Has It All started on Twitter with a handful of

Aknowledgements

followers in 2015. Thank you to those of you who have been there all along. You know who you are. To my Facebook followers, especially those who comment and play along, I see you and you see each other. Let's keep going until there is nothing left to laugh at.

To my genius agent Sarah Ballard, I love that you get it and did from the start. Thank you also to Eli and Liv, for doing all the things. Thank you to Fiona Lensvelt from Unbound who first approached me and encouraged me to write this book. Thank you to all my editors for doing the important stuff to make this book happen (especially total legend, Marissa Constantinou), Matthew Clayton and to everyone at Unbound for being so lovely to work with.

Last of all, if you've got this far, well done, and thanks for reading (in Caitlin Moran's words) 'this exasperating, time-wasting bullshit'.

Further Reading

I am not the first, and won't be the last, to flip the script. This final section introduces you to a range of other authors and artists who turn the tables on the patriarchy, offering new insights and covering different ground. As I said in the Foreword, there is, unfortunately, plenty of material to go round. Thank you to supporters of this book for bringing to my attention work I hadn't come across before. This is very much optional reading, because I do not want to add to the loads I talk about in this book: the mental load, the emotional load, the kindness load, the beauty load, the humour load, the sportswoman's load, the historical load, the women at work load and the language load.

Theatre
The Taming of the Shrew by the Royal Shakespeare Company (2019), a gender-swapped production of Shakespeare's classic
Beauty and the Beast by Fat Rascal Theatre, a gender-swapped performance at the King's Head Theatre, Islington
Until the Lions, choreographed by Akram Khan, a dance version of Indian classical stories that puts women at the centre of an epic Indian story – a position that is typically reserved for men

Further Reading

Film

Barbie, directed by Greta Gerwig

Oppressed Majority, written and directed by Eléonore Pourriat

I Am Not an Easy Man, written and directed by Eléonore Pourriat

Jue wang zhu fu ('*Better Man*'), directed by Qi Zhang

Art

The Hawkeye Initiative, drawing male superheroes in the poses traditionally associated with female ones

Jim C. Hines posing like the women shown on the covers of urban fantasy novels

Kevin Bolk's *Avengers Assemble* poster, in which all the male characters are posed like Scarlett Johansson's *Black Widow*

'Helmut Newton As Seen By Hani Hape', a series of photographs recreating fashion photographer Newton's female nudes, replacing them with images of men

Australian comedy duo Bondi Hipsters subverting Miranda Kerr's *GQ* photoshoot

Jennifer Lopez's video for the single 'I Luh Ya Papi'

Social media

@Clarabellecwb on TikTok flips gender and/or race

@seiten.verkehrt on Instagram asks what happens if we simply reverse stereotypes and sexist patterns

@tiffstevenson on Twitter parodies the way male authors write about women

#FlipItToTestIt on Twitter, and the TED Talk with the same name, from Kristen Pressner

Fiction

Egalia's Daughters: A Satire of the Sexes by Gerd Brantenberg

Gender-swapped Fairy Tales by Karrie Fransman and Jonathan Plackett

Further Reading

Gender-swapped Greek Myths by Karrie Fransman and Jonathan Plackett
The Power by Naomi Alderman
Rogue Princess by B. R. Myers
The Princess Will Save You by Sarah Henning
Travelers Along the Way by Aminah Mae Safi
Fairy Tales of the Sisters Grimm, transcribed by Gisela Qasim
Fa La La by Michelle Cornish
Violet the Pilot by Steve Breen
Sam Johnson and the Blue Ribbon Quilt by Lisa Campbell Ernst
If Men Could Menstruate by Gloria Steinem

Books that put women back into history

These are the books I talk about in Chapter 7: Men's History, firstly listed in historical order and then grouped by theme and by geography. You'll notice as you read about these books that some words are used to describe women's place in history again and again: invisible, lost, secret, omission, ignored, forgotten, untold, silenced, written out, oversight, unrecognised, destroyed, unheralded, unrewarded, unsung, missing and hidden. Meanwhile, men in history have been visible, included, told, seen, acknowledged, written in, recognised, heralded, rewarded, celebrated and obvious. To put it metaphorically, they have been spreading their historical legs and taking up all the space.

So who hid women's history and why? The women (and men) who wrote the books listed below noticed that half of history was missing, so they looked for it, found it and wrote about it. Cometh the hour, cometh the woman (or man)!

Eve: How The Female Body Drove 200 Million Years of Human Evolution by Cat Bohannon

In the foreword to my book I talked about the injustices I have felt over my lifetime motivating me to write *Flipping Patriarchy*. But the omission the author describes in this book puts my 'it's not fair!'

Further Reading

moments into perspective. Women have been written out of TWO HUNDRED MILLION YEARS of human evolution. Let that sink in. This book is a revision and a corrective, answering questions about human evolution that should have been answered decades ago.

Lady Sapiens: Breaking Stereotypes About Prehistoric Women by **Thomas Cirotteau, Jennifer Kerner and Eric Pincas**
It probably won't surprise you to learn that prehistoric women didn't get much of a mention by historians for a whopping 150 years. Before *Lady Sapiens* was written, we were lost in cliches about prehistoric man doing the exciting stuff like hunting, inventing and drawing while we looked after the baby prehistorics and cleaned the cave, presumably smiling. The researchers behind this book have rewritten prehistory using groundbreaking excavation methods.

Pandora's Jar: Women in the Greek Myths by **Natalie Haynes**
Why do you have to bring gender into everything? is something I ask myself after getting towards the end of writing this book. *How can you shoehorn gender into Greek myths?* The answer is, because the topic is already gendered. Pre-gendered. Greek myths have been told largely by men through the ages. Unsurprisingly this means a large bias towards stories of male gods, man monsters and men humans. Natalie Haynes redresses the imbalance by telling the stories of Hera, Athena and Artemis, and of Clytemnestra, Jocasta, Eurydice and Penelope.

A History of the Roman Empire in 21 Women by **Emma Southon**
A viral 2022 TikTok trend revealed that men think about the Roman Empire a lot, even many times a day. Could these thoughts of long-ago battles, generals and emperors be distracting men from the important things, such as remembering to top up the school dinner balance and feeding the rabbits? This important book flips the script; the Roman business owners, poets, leaders and saints are all women. A different legacy of Rome with new narratives and legends.

Further Reading

The Very Secret Sex Lives of Medieval Women: An Inside Look at Women & Sex in Medieval Times by **Rosalie Gilbert**

Were medieval women real people? Or did they just exist in relation to their husband's desires? Is it even possible to find out? It turns out that we know more about female sexuality during this period than it was first thought. Rosalie Gilbert reveals the ins and outs of sexual practices in medieval times, re-inserting woman back into the story.

The Hidden History of Women's Ordination: Female Clergy in the Medieval West by **Gary Macy**

Gary Macy uncovers the real history of women's ordination during the first 1200 years of Christianity. He discovers that, contrary to popular belief, women held a variety of roles in the Christian church during this time. This book is important because it disrupts the common argument that women have never been officially ordained and aren't capable of it. The author's research has the potential to change the contemporary debate about women's role in the church.

Femina: A New History of the Middle Ages, Through the Women Written Out of It by **Janina Ramirez**

Women of the Middle Ages were scammed! They were pro-actively removed from history, with the word 'FEMINA' written beside the names of influential women in historical records. The work of these women was destroyed and replaced with new, manipulated versions of historical records. This book tells a new history of the period through the women erased from the past.

The Real Valkyrie: The Hidden History of Viking Warrior Women by **Nancy Marie Brown**

Imagine the surprise of male scholars when they found out that a renowned Viking warrior was actually a woman! Nancy Marie Brown reinvents Valkyrie's history, revealing that Viking women had a much more prominent role than previously thought.

Further Reading

Warriors, Queens and Intellectuals: 36 Great Women Before 1400 by Joyce E. Salisbury

Joyce E. Salisbury unearths the history of thirty-six powerful women of their times, revealing that women were not just mothers, seducers and maidens. Far from it. Some of the women she describes were manipulative and murderous. Many great women before 1400 have been lost to historical bias. The author invites us to imagine what we are missing when only half the story is being told.

The Hidden Lives of Tudor Women by Elizabeth Norton

Another historic period and another hidden history of half the population. And it turns out that this invisible population of women was powerful and dominant in a way not seen in centuries before. Elizabeth Norton writes about the real lives of Tudor women through the stories of royal Tudors, a wet nurse and a peasant girl. This book reveals that there was a lot more to Tudor women than elaborate hats and triangular skirts.

How to Be a Renaissance Woman: The Untold History of Beauty and Creativity by Jill Burke

This important book about the world of the Renaissance Woman uncovers the previously invisible history of beauty and creativity during this influential period. Women of the Renaissance did not just feature in men's paintings looking virtuous and submissive. These often silenced and forgotten women were powerful artists, artisans, aristocrats and businesswomen, gaining influence in the ruthless world of the court. This fresh, women-centred look at the period also invites the reader to trace contemporary beauty ideals back to these extraordinary times.

The Pocket: A Hidden History of Women's Lives, 1660–1900 by Barbara Burnam and Ariana Fennetaux

Telling the story of women's lives through the tie-on pocket, this book explores the hidden social history of women's lives. The tie-on pocket was a small, sometimes embroidered bag tied around

Further Reading

the waist that women used to carry their personal possessions during the 1700s. Unfortunately, we still need to buy updated versions of these little pouches today (think rectangular crossbody bags) to carry our phones in, because women's clothes often don't have pockets. And if we do have pockets, they usually aren't big enough for our enormous mobiles, designed for men's larger hands. The personal pocket was, and still is, political.

Pirate Women: The Princesses, Prostitutes and Privateers Who Ruled the Seven Seas **by Laura Sook Duncombe, Hillary Huber, et al.**
Largely ignored until now, the stories of the brave pirate women who sailed the Seven Seas alongside man pirates who they often commanded are explored in this book. I love the way the author has the ovaries to tell the stories of legendary women who may not have existed. Because why not? History is packed full of male figures who may be representative rather than real: think Robin Hood, King Arthur, Pythagoras, Homer and William Tell to name but a few.

Women of the Durham Coalfield in the 19th Century: Hannah's Story **by Margaret Hedley**
Before this book, very little was written about the women of the Durham Coalfields. Their important role in the Industrial Revolution has been almost entirely written out of history. This book re-inserts women back into the history of this period which was characterised by often appalling conditions. The author describes their efforts as heroic, drawing attention to the huge sacrifices women made to ensure their miner husbands lived in healthy, happy homes.

The Women of Rothschild: The Untold Story of the World's Most Famous Dynasty **by Natalie Livingstone, Francesca Waters, et al.**
Guess which half of this famous family's story has been largely ignored? This book traces the extraordinary stories of Rothschild women throughout the nineteenth century. The Rothschild family,

Further Reading

although important in historical terms, is just one renowned family. Imagine all the other famous, wealthy and powerful families in the world and the hidden stories of women waiting to be told.

Real Women of the Regency: Romance, Affairs, Fashion, Authors to Actresses and Women Leaders by Leah Gail

More overooked women feature in this book about the Regency period. The author explores the work of the women who made important contributions to their fields in times of radical change and political upheaval. She focuses particularly on the previously invisible lives of lesbians and Black women of the Regency period.

The Five: The Untold Lives of the Women Killed by Jack the Ripper by Hallie Rubenhold, Louise Brealey, et al.

This groundbreaking biography of five named women – Polly, Annie, Elizabeth, Catherine and Mary-Jane –tells the previously untold stories of those killed by Jack the Ripper. While his name has become widely known, little has been known about the lives of his victims until now. In this much needed corrective, distinguished historian Halle Rubenhold gives these women back their voice.

Wifedom: Mrs Orwell's Invisible Life by Anna Funder

This book uncovers the role of Eileen O'Shaughnessy in George Orwell's life who remained strangely absent from his biographies. Anna Funder, an author herself, finds out why and how Eileen O'Shaughnessy was written out of the story when she clearly played a significant role in his husband's success, from improving his writing skills to actually saving his life. This book will appeal to all women who feel their efforts go unnoticed, especially those who marry a writer and become a Mrs.

The Girls Who Stepped Out of Line: Untold Stories of the Women Who Changed the Course of World War II by Mari K. Eder

This book tells the untold stories of the unheralded, unrewarded and

Further Reading

unsung women who shaped the events of World War II. The author reveals the previously hidden contribution of fifteen brave and hard-working women of the Greatest Generation. I love the way this book corrects the narrative that only men can be war heroes.

Confinement: The Hidden History of Maternal Bodies in Nineteenth-Century Britain by Jessica Cox
Although women's central role during the nineteenth century was seen as producing and rearing children, the pregnant and postnatal body is mysteriously missing from the written records of this era. This revised history of pregnancy and motherhood corrects this oversight, exploring the real experiences of women during pregnancy, childbirth and breastfeeding. She also reveals what it was like to have a miscarriage, lose a child and have an unwanted pregnancy during this period. This important contribution to the history of the female body reminds us of the incredible advances in maternal medicine and of the dangers of pseudoscience in health today.

Vanguard: How Black Women Broke Barriers, Won the Vote, and Insisted on Equality for All by Martha S. Jones
Historian Martha S. Jones retells the political history of African American women through the suffrage period. She excavates the stories of Black women who fought racism and sexism – Maria Stewart, Frances Ellen Watkins Harper, Fannie Lou Hamer and others – to win the vote and secure rights for all, correcting the common narrative that centres on white women.

A History of the World with the Women Put Back In by Kursten Luckerand and Ute Daenschel
This ambitious meta-book puts women back into history, telling the stories of the women who stayed at home, those who went to war and those who stopped war. The authors write 'once upon a time, history was written by men, for men and about men.' I like their optimism and hope that history today will be written by everyone,

Further Reading

for everyone and about everyone. With men quite possibly taking a back seat for a while to allow women to catch up.

Forgotten Women: The Women Who Shaped and Were Erased from Our History by Zing Tsjeng

Another far-reaching work covering world history rediscovers, retells and reinstates the lives of nearly 200 notable, but forgotten, women from the New Stone Age to modern times. Respect to Tsjeng for choosing just 200 women from the last ten thousand years. An interview with the author reveals that she spent eight or nine hours a day in the British library searching for women's works that were out of print.[1] I hope someone cooked her dinner for her when she returned home from work.

On This Day She: Putting Women Back Into History, One Day at a Time by Tania Hershman, Ailsa Holland, et al.

Like the two books above, this work puts influential women back into history, giving a voice to those unfairly written out of history. Covering politicians, rebels, innovators, creatives, scientists and murderers, the authors take on the challenge of biased men's history one day at a time.

Bloody Brilliant Women: The Pioneers, Revolutionaries and Geniuses Your History Teacher Forgot to Mention by Cathy Newman

We've all heard of the great men of history; the male monarchs, men rulers and boy scientists. Focusing on modern Britain, Cathy Newman looks instead at the lives of great women who changed the course of history, making careers for themselves and subverting long-held beliefs about women's role in society.

A Black Women's History of the United States by Daina Ramey Berry and Kali Nicole Gross

This important book re-inserts Black women into American history, emphasising African American women's ability to forge their

Further Reading

own communities at the same time as fighting many centuries of oppression. The authors start with a history of the first African women living in the US and end with present-day African American women. Perhaps a future edition will celebrate the first African American, Asian American and first daughter of immigrants to become US president. This book is an essential corrective to the ubiquitous White Man's History of the United States that pretends to be universal, comprehensive and unbiased.

She Speaks: Women's Speeches That Changed the World, from Pankhurst to Greta by Yvette Cooper
Books about the greatest speeches of all time give the impression that brilliant oratory is a man thing. Many of these books would be better titled 'He Speaks' or 'Male Oratory', given the content. Cooper's book reframes public speaking as decidedly female, drawing on talented orators such as Boudica, Greta Thunberg, Chimamanda Adichie and Malala Yousafzai to show how women's speeches have inspired, transformed and shaped world history.

Little Leaders: Bold Women in Black History by Vashti Harrison
This illustrated book celebrates forty boundary-breaking Black women in world history, educating and inspiring readers at the same time. The author tells the stories of both famous and less well-known figures, such as Nurse Mary Seacole, Politician Diane Abbott, Mathematician Katherine Johnson and Singer Shirley Bassey. Buy this children's book for your son, nephew or grandson. We can teach girls to be leaders, but we must also inspire boys to be followers. This book shows them the way.

A History of Britain in 21 Women by Jenni Murray
More revolutionary, previously unrecognised women are featured in this book of British history by Jenni Murray. This time, the lives of twenty-one trailblazing women tell a new inspirational and hopeful story of Britain. Perhaps Jenni Murray herself, alongside some of the

Further Reading

other authors mentioned in this section, will feature in a similar book in future for her phenomenal contribution to British broadcasting history after presenting Radio 4's *Woman's Hour* from 1987 until 2020.

100 Nasty Women of History: Brilliant, badass and completely fearless women everyone should know by Hannah Jewell, Rachael Verkui, et al.

100 nasty women? Surely not! Hannah Jewell reveals that actually, women from the past didn't just float about in pretty dresses waiting to be painted, or have sons. Some women, perhaps even more than a hundred, were pretty horrible. This warts-and-all book reveals just some of the women who male historians forgot, or chose not, to mention.

The Women Who Made Modern Economics by Rachel Reeves

Another revelatory book about women who have been overlooked and their stories untold, this time focusing on the hugely influential sphere of economics. The UK chancellor, Rachel Reeves, sets out the economic theories of influential women such as Harriet Martineau, Mary Paley Marshall, Joan Robinson, Janet Yellen, Gita Gopinath and Christine Lagarde.

Fantastically Great Women Who Changed The World by Kate Pankhurst

In this book, Kate Pankhurst writes about some of the brilliant but overlooked women who changed the world. Now a musical, this stunning collection of facts and illustrations appeals to both adults and children. This book deserves to be read by boys as well as girls, to remind them that history does not just belong to them.

Her Story: 50 Women and Girls Who Shook the World by Katherine Halligan

Further Reading

Another illustrated book for children focuses on the girlhoods of fifty formidable women from around the world. Designed to educate and inspire, it celebrates pioneers in their various fields.

The Philosopher Queens by Rebecca Buxton and Lisa Whiting
What, women did philosophy too? This phenomenal book centres twenty philosophers you may never heard of, including Hypatia, Arendt, Oluwole and Young, whose work has had an enormous, but as yet unsung, impact on the way we think today. Move over Plato, Kant, Nietzsche and Descartes. She thinks, therefore she is.

A Lesbian History of Britain: Love and Sex Between Women Since 1500 by Rebecca Jennings
Female desire in Britain is the focus of this much-needed history book. The author uses a variety of sources to tell the extraordinary stories of both well-known and lesser known lesbian women. The author also examines the changing representations and cultural attitudes towards love and sex between women throughout the ages. We need more books like this to counter the histories of Britain written by male heterosexuals framing women as objects and possessions: wives, daughters, procreators and victims. In this book, woman is the subject.

A History of Women in Medicine: Cunning Women, Physicians, Witches by Sinead Spearing
We all know about witches, they come out at Halloween with their pointy hats, broomsticks and black hats. Harmless enough surely, except when they are turning people into mice, lizards or upside-down cockerels. But did you know that female physicians who were once held in high esteem were subsequently demonised as witches by the Church? The author sets the record straight, separating women in medicine from the derogatory and dangerous words, like cunning, evil and hysteria, used to describe and discredit them.

Further Reading

Warrior Queens and Quiet Revolutionaries: How Women (Also) Build the World by Kate Mosse
Unheard and under-heard, nearly one thousand courageous women are celebrated in this book about unsung heroes from the past. The warrior queens and quiet revolutionaries featured in this book all commanded their field, from the sea to the screen.

Normal Women: 900 Years of Making History by Philippa Gregory
Women of Great Britain weren't all inventors, queens or heroes. Some were quite ordinary. In this book Phillipa Gregory explores the lives of what she describes as 'normal' women, providing a counterbalance to the many history books about working-class men, the working man and ordinary men.

Difficult Women: A History of Feminism in 11 Fights by Helen Lewis
This is not a feel-good book. Just as male figures in history can be complex, problematic and divisive, so of course can women. Helen Lewis introduces feminist trailblazers whose lives and actions have been conveniently forgotten by male historians who prefer historical women to be well behaved, tame and one-dimensional.

Women Sailors and Sailors' Women by David Cordingly
This book reveals that the sea was not only a male domain. The author has unearthed stories of young women wearing men's clothes and working on ships with male sailors for years, without anyone knowing. Although penned by a male author, this book is actually well written and researched. You go, boy!

The Story of Art Without Men by Katy Hessel
What a title! A tribute to women artists, this revisionist history book re-inserts dismissed or overlooked women into the story of art. The author shines a light on women's creativity and the impact it has had on the world.

Further Reading

Why Have There Been No Great Women Artists? **by Linda Nochlin and Catherine Grant**
Also on the subject of women artists is Linda Nochlin's landmark work challenging the male lens through which art has traditionally been viewed. Provocative and witty, this book challenges the male-coded ideas of genius and greatness.

Magnificent Women and Flying Machines **by Sally Smith**
This book tells the untold stories of the magnificent women who flew in the face of traditional stereotypes. Focusing on the first women to achieve heights in different forms of aviation, from hot air ballooning to space travel, Sally Smith has written an authoritative and entertaining account of Britain's fearless women of the skies.

Wanderers: A History of Women Walking **by Kerri Andrews**
And now to the land. Kerri Andrews' book tells the intimate stories of ten women wanderers from the past three hundred years who found walking to be essential to their sense of self. The book offers insights beyond pathfinding, showing us a new ways of seeing and becoming ourselves.

Where are the Women?: A Guide to an Imagined Scotland **by Sara Sheridan**
Imagine if women were honoured in statues and on street signs in Scotland, not just in the cities but in the hills and valleys too. The author creates an alternative Scotland, gender-swapping famous statues, station names and monuments to create a fictional world where great historical women are front and centre of the streetscape. By honouring real women who have achieved incredible things, Sheriden reinstates little-known female figures into the history of Scotland.

Where There's Muck, There's Bras: Lost Stories of the Amazing Women of the North **by Kate Fox**
Similarly, Kate Fox reinserts forgotten women into the history of

Further Reading

the North of England. This wide-reaching, original and funny book shows how forgotten women from as far back as the Iron Age paved the way for modern stars such as Victora Wood and Betty Boothroyd. *Where There's Muck, There's Bras* is a welcome corrective to the many male-centred, and quite possibly turgid, histories of the North.

Inspired By

Here is a list of websites and articles that have inspired some of the gender-flipped sections in this book. Where real-world material has been drawn from in the text, I have mentioned that the sources can be found in this section.

Nice Women
'The Gentleman's Code', Jack and Jil Live, 2013, www.jacknjillive.com/2013/10/the-gentlemans-code/
'The Gentleman's Code: 11 Unspoken Rules for the Modern Man', Gentlemen's Digest, 21 December 2023, www.gentlemens-digest.com/lifestyle/the-gentlemans-code-11-unspoken-rules-for-the-modern-man/

Heard the One About a Man Trying to Park a Car?
'25 Groom Speech Jokes That Guarantee Laughs', Hitched, 17 January 2024, www.hitched.co.uk/wedding-planning/organising-and-planning/groom-speech-jokes/
'Mother In-Law Jokes', Funktion Events, 12 June 2023, www.funktionevents.co.uk/stag-do/blog/mother-in-law-jokes
'110 Sexist Jokes To Make You Laugh (Men & Women)', The (mostly) Simple Life, www.themostlysimplelife.com/jokes/best-sexist-jokes/

Inspired By

'Funny Sexist Jokes!', Keep Laughing Forever, www.keeplaughing forever.com/sexist-jokes

'60 Funny Blonde Jokes You Should Probably Never Say Out Loud', Best Life, 28 March 2024, www.bestlifeonline.com/blonde-jokes/

'215 Best Yo Mama Jokes of All Time', Best Life, 26 September 2024, www.bestlifeonline.com/yo-mama-jokes/

Men in Sport

'Premier League chief executive under fire for sexist emails', *Guardian*, 11 May 2014, www.theguardian.com/football/2014/may/11/richard-scudamore-under-fire-over-sexist-emails

'"KEEP HER OFF YOUR SHAFT" Sexist emails exchanged between Premier League boss Richard Scudamore and fined lawyer', *Sun*, 14 June 2016, www.thesun.co.uk/news/1283431/sexist-emails-ex changed-between-premier-league-boss-richard-scudamore-and-fined-lawyer/

'Richard Scudamore', Wikipedia, en.wikipedia.org/wiki/Richard_Scuda more

'Premier League chief Richard Scudamore sorry for "lack of judge-ment" after leak of sexist emails', *Independent*, 12 May 2014, www.independent.co.uk/sport/football/news/premier-league-chief-richard-scudamore-sorry-for-lack-of-judgement-after-leak-of-sexist-emails-9352616.html

'Premier League chief Richard Scudamore forced to apologise for sending sexist emails', Mail Online, 11 May 2014, www.dailymail.co.uk/sport/article-2625464/Premier-League-chief-forced-apolo gise-sending-sexist-emails-referring-women-joking-breasts.html

'EXCLUSIVE: England football supremo Richard Scudamore made sexist slurs in a string of emails to soccer pals', *Mirror*, 10 May 2014, www.mirror.co.uk/news/uk-news/premier-league-boss-richard-scudamore-3524857

'Richard Scudamore: no further action over sexist emails', 4 News, 19

Inspired By

May 2014, www.channel4.com/news/committee-to-meet-over-premier-league-chiefs-sexist-emails

'Richard Scudamore under pressure to resign over sexist emails', *Guardian*, 16 May 2024, www.theguardian.com/football/2014/may/16/richard-scudamore-premier-league-sexist-emails-untenable

'Richard Scudamore under pressure to resign over sexist emails: Premier League chief executive will face "no further action" over sexist emails', *Independent*, 20 May 2014, www.independent.co.uk/sport/football/news/richard-scudamore-emails-premier-league-chief-executive-will-face-no-further-action-over-sending-sexist-emails-9398984.html

'Richard Scudamore will accept £5m departure bonus from Premier League', *Guardian*, 15 November 2018, www.theguardian.com/football/2018/nov/15/premier-league-5m-richard-scudamore-gift

'Richard Scudamore accepts £5m departure bonus from Premier League clubs', *Mirror*, 15 November 2018, www.mirror.co.uk/sport/football/news/richard-scudamore-accepts-5m-departure-13594560

'Premier League: Richard Scudamore accepts £5m departure bonus from all 20 clubs', *Independent*, 15 November 2018, www.independent.co.uk/sport/football/premier-league/premier-league-richard-scudamore-payoff-ps5million-how-much-when-epl-a8635261.html

'UK Attitudes Towards Women in Sport 2023', Insure4Sport, 28 February 2023, www.insure4sport.co.uk/blog/uk-attitudes-towards-women-in-sport/

'From ball girls to birthday cake – tennis sure has form when it comes to sexism', *Standard*, 11 May 2023, www.standard.co.uk/lifestyle/madrid-open-ball-girl-outfits-lacoste-birthday-cake-sexism-b1079862.html

'Madrid Open "ball girls" outfits spark sexism row', *Independent*, 9 May 2023, www.independent.co.uk/sport/tennis/madrid-open-ball-girls-outfits-sexism-b2335413.html

Inspired By

'Madrid Open sexism scandals blow hole in tennis equality myth', *Telegraph*, 9 May 2023, www.telegraph.co.uk/tennis/2023/05/09/madrid-open-sexism-scandal-blows-hole-tennis-equality-myth/

'"We are still fighting": London 2012 silver medalist Lizzie Deignan says sexism is still a problem in cycling', *Independent*, 3 May 2018, www.independent.co.uk/sport/cycling/sexism-cycling-lizzie-deignan-tour-de-yorkshire-women-a8334991.html

'Cycling Weekly apologises after printing sexist picture caption that read "token attractive woman" next to female cyclist', *Independent*, 1 September 2017, www.independent.co.uk/sport/cycling/cycling-weekly-sexist-sexism-picture-caption-token-attractive-woman-apology-female-cyclist-a7923721.html

Men's History

'D. H. Lawrence Quotes' and 'Herbert Simon Quotes', quotefancy.com

'Aldous Huxley Quotes', brainyquote.com

Notes

Foreword

1. Jean-Paul Sartre, *Dirty Hands*, Premiered at Théâtre Antoine, Paris, 1948.

Introduction

1. Katherine Rothschild, 'Satirical feminism and the Reparative Tweet: a discourse analysis of the gendered language of @manwhohasitall', Taylor & Francis Online, 28 June 2021, www.tandfonline.com/doi/abs/10.1080/14680777.2021.1946581

Nice Women

1. Kristen Roupenian, 'Cat Person', *New Yorker*, 24 December 2017.
2. Emma Gill, 'Sainsbury's kids' slogan tops slammed for reinforcing attitudes that "endanger women"', *Manchester Evening News,* 12 October 2021, www.manchestereveningnews.co.uk/whats-on/family-kids-news/sainsburys-kids-slogan-tops-slammed-21821026
3. Gloria Oladipo, 'Newspaper deletes glowing obituary of Utah man accused of killing his family', *Guardian*, 18 January 2023, www.theguardian.com/us-news/2023/jan/18/utah-newspaper-the-spectrum-obituary-man-accused-killing-family

Notes

4. Alex Hammer, 'Warped obituary for Utah murder-suicide . . .', *Daily Mail*, 16 January 2023, www.dailymail.co.uk/news/article-11639109/Warped-obituary-Utah-man-murdered-wife-five-kids-says-great-dad.html

Dad's To-do List

1. Dad Marketing, 'Playtex Baby Forgets Half of Its Customers', 6 February 2023, dadmarketing.com/2023/02/06/playtex-baby-forgets-half-of-its-customers/

Not Just a Pretty Beard

1. Daniel Cox, Beatrice Lee and Dana Popky, 'How Prevalent Is Pornography?', Institute for Family Studies, 3 May 2022, ifstudies.org/blog/how-prevalent-is-pornography

2. Stewart Lee, *Comedy Vehicle*, Episode 3, Series 6, 5 April 2014, BBC.

3. Molly Clayton, 'Michael Caine's secret to a long and happy life at 90: Stop eating between meals, wear trainers and take a younger wife,' Mail online, 24 September 2023, www.dailymail.co.uk/tvshowbiz/article-12553287/Michael-Caines-secret-long-happy-life-90-Stop-eating-meals-wear-trainers-younger-wife.html

Heard the One About a Man Trying to Park a Car?

1. Mónica Romero-Sánchez, Hugo Carretero-Dios, Jesús L. Megías, Miguel Moya, Thomas E. Ford, 'Sexist Humor and Rape Proclivity: The Moderating Role of Joke Teller Gender and Severity of Sexual Assault', Violence Against Women, DOI: 10.1177/1077801216654017, 6 July 2016.

2. Terry Pratchett, 'An SFBC exclusive interview with Terry Pratchett', www.lspace.org/about-terry/interviews/sfbc.html

3. Jaclyn Andrea Reed, 'The Caustic Pen Is Mightiest: A Tradition of Female Satire in the Novels of Jane Austen, Ivy Compton-

Notes

Burnett, and Muriel Spark', University of Denver, digital commons.du.edu/cgi/viewcontent.cgi?article=1996&context=etd

4. Keiran Southern, 'Steve Coogan: Comedians should punch up, not down', *Belfast Telegraph*, 26 October 2019, www.belfasttelegraph.co.uk/entertainment/film-tv/news/steve-coogan-comedians-should-punch-up-not-down/38632680.html

5. Paul Simpson, *On the Discourse of Satire: Towards a stylistic model of satirical humor*, John Benjamins Publishing, Amsterdam, November 2003.

6. Ibid.

7. Judy Brady, 'The '70s Feminist Manifesto That's Still a Must-Read Today', *The Cut*, November 2017, www.thecut.com/2017/11/i-want-a-wife-by-judy-brady-syfers-new-york-mag-1971.html

8. Giverny Masso, 'Men earned 60% more than women at last year's Edinburgh Fringe, study claims', *The Stage*, 26 July 2019, www.thestage.co.uk/news/men-earned-60-more-than-women-at-last-years-edinburgh-fringe-study-claims

9. Chortle, 'Revealed: Just how male-dominated TV comedy writing is', 23 May 2018, www.chortle.co.uk/news/2018/05/22/40031/revealed:_just_how_male-dominated_tv_comedy_writing_is

10. 'Women in comedy', Wikipedia, en.wikipedia.org/wiki/Women_in_comedy

Men in Sport

1. Kevin Lincoln, 'London's Goofy Mayor Likened Women Volleyballers To "Glistening Wet Otters"', *Buzzfeed*, 30 July 2012, www.buzzfeed.com/ktlincoln/londons-goofy-mayor-likened-women-volleyballers-t

2. Anna Kessel, 'How The Telegraph is breaking new ground for women's sport', The Game Changers, 24 September 2019, www.fearlesswomen.co.uk/thegamechangers/anna-kessel

3. Becky Grey, 'Sportswomen share experiences of sexism and the

Notes

reasons they do not report it', BBC Sport, 14 August 2020, www.bbc.co.uk/sport/53593465

4. 'Girls as young as five years old don't feel that they belong in sport', Women in Sport, 9 March 2023, womeninsport.org/news/girls-as-young-as-five-years-old-dont-feel-that-they-belong-in-sport/

5. 'Misogyny in sports', Wikipedia, en.wikipedia.org/wiki/Misogyny_in_sports#Demeaning_language

6. Suzanne Wrack, 'Gianni Infantino urges women to "pick the right battles" in equal pay fight', *Guardian*, www.theguardian.com/football/2023/aug/18/gianni-infantino-urges-women-to-pick-the-right-battles-in-equal-pay-fight

Mister Chairwoman

1. Joseph Epstein, 'Is There a Doctor in the White House? Not if You Need an M.D.', *Wall Street Journal*, 11 December 2020, www.wsj.com/articles/is-there-a-doctor-in-the-white-house-not-if-you-need-an-m-d-11607727380

2. Rebecca Ratcliffe, 'Nobel scientist Tim Hunt: female scientists cause trouble for men in labs', *Guardian*, 10 June 2015, www.theguardian.com/uk-news/2015/jun/10/nobel-scientist-tim-hunt-female-scientists-cause-trouble-for-men-in-labs

3. Carmen Rios, 'Calling Grown Women "Girls" Is Sexist As Hell – Here Are 4 Reasons Why', Everyday Feminism, 30 June 2015, www.everydayfeminism.com/2015/06/grown-women-are-not-girls/

4. '12 times famous women perfectly shut down sexist interview questions', 5 March 2023, www.indy100.com/celebrities/famous-women-sexist-interview-questions

5. Kalyeena Makortoff, '"Unacceptable": Aviva CEO hits back at shareholder sexism', *Guardian*, 12 May 2022, www.theguardian.com/inequality/2022/may/11/used-to-it-aviva-ceo-responds-after-sexist-comments-at-agm

Notes

6. 'Nadia Lim opens up on why she is speaking out against Simon Henry's derogatory "Eurasian fluff" comments', *NZ Herald*, 5 May 2022, www.nzherald.co.nz/business/nadia-lim-opens-up-on-why-she-is-speaking-out-against-simon-henrys-derogatory-eurasian-fluff-comments/5FMP4PPWCPGHA6JAPRSFFFGE4U/

7. Simon Mills and Amanda Platell, 'What DO men think as they gaze at a woman? Two writers give their brutally honest verdicts on how people size up the opposite sex', *Daily Mail*, 4 August 2023, www.dailymail.co.uk/femail/article-12371429/What-men-think-gaze-woman-Two-writers-brutally-honest-verdicts-people-size-opposite-sex.html

8. 'Banned Words', *Telegraph*, 23 January 2018, www.telegraph.co.uk/style-book/banned-words/

9 'Sea-change in UK as women make up nearly 40% of FTSE 100 top table roles', Department for Business, Energy & Industrial Strategy, 22 February 2023, www.gov.uk/government/news/sea-change-in-uk-boardrooms-as-women-make-up-nearly-40-of-ftse-100-top-table-roles

10. Jennifer Rankin, 'Fewer women leading FTSE firms than men called John', *Guardian*, 6 March 2015, www.theguardian.com/business/2015/mar/06/johns-davids-and-ians-outnumber-female-chief-executives-in-ftse-100

11. 'New TUC poll: 2 in 3 young women have experienced sexual harassment, bullying or verbal abuse at work', The TUC, 12 May 2023, www.tuc.org.uk/news/new-tuc-poll-2-3-young-women-have-experienced-sexual-harassment-bullying-or-verbal-abuse-work

12. Daniel Woolfson '"Men are nervous working with women" after string of harassment claims, says ex-Tesco chair John Allan', *Telegraph*, 18 June 2023, www.telegraph.co.uk/business/2023/06/18/jonh-allan-ex-tesco-chair-men-nervous-working-with-women/

13. Pamela Duncan, Carmen Aguilar García and Jasper Jolly, 'Women still paid less than men at four out of five employers in

Notes

Great Britain', *Guardian*, 4 April 2023, www.theguardian.com/world/2023/apr/05/women-paid-less-than-men-four-out-of-five--employers-uk-gender-pay-gap

14. Derek Thompson, 'Women Are More Responsible With Money, Studies Show', *Atlantic*, 31 January 2011, www.theatlantic.com/business/archive/2011/01/women-are-more-responsible-with-money-studies-show/70539/

15. Eleanor Rathbone, *The Case for Family Allowances*, Penguin, 1940.

16. Ruth Lister and Jason Strelitz, *Why Money Matters: Family income, poverty and children's lives*, Save the Children, 2008, pp. 115–24.

17. 'About Maternity Discrimination', Pregnant Then Screwed, www.pregnantthenscrewed.com/about-maternity-discrimination/

18. 'Stories', Pregnant Then Screwed, www.pregnantthenscrewed.com/category/stories/

19. 'Gender segregation contributes to sexual harassment in the workplace', Open Access Government, 13 May 2022, www.openaccessgovernment.org/gender-segregation-contributes-sexual-harassment-workplace-inequality/135517/#:~:text=Individuals

20. Emine Saner, 'Why women won't ask for a pay rise', *Guardian*, 27 August 2010, www.theguardian.com/lifeandstyle/2010/aug/27/women-wont-ask-pay-rises

21. Andrew Griffiths, 'Revealed: The worst explanations for not appointing women to FTSE company boards', Department for Business, Energy & Strategy, www.gov.uk/government/news/revealed-the-worst-explanations-for-not-appointing-women-to-ftse-company-boards

Men's History

1. Oscar Wilde, 'The Critic as Artist', *Intentions*, 1891.

2. Credit to a Facebook follower, who is quite possibly a historian, for 'Wars and Wanking'.

Notes

The Clitionary

1. 'Oxford's Dictionary is Spreading Misogyny Online', Girls Globe, 31 July 2019, www.girlsglobe.org/2019/07/31/oxfords-dictionary-is-spreading-misogyny-online/
2. 'Dictionaries, dick-tionaries and dyketionaries', Debuk Wordpress, 30 June 2015, debuk.wordpress.com/2015/06/30/dictionaries-dick-tionaries-and-dyketionaries/
3. 'Transcript: Donald Trump's Taped Comments About Women', *New York Times*, 8 October 2016, www.nytimes.com/2016/10/08/us/donald-trump-tape-transcript.html

Further Reading

1. 'Finding Forgotten Women in the Collection | User Stories' Knowledge Matters blog, The British Library, 30 June 2023, blogs.bl.uk/living-knowledge/2023/06/finding-forgotten-women-in-the-collection-user-stories.html

Unbound is the world's first crowdfunding publisher, established in 2011.

We believe that wonderful things can happen when you clear a path for people who share a passion. That's why we've built a platform that brings together readers and authors to crowdfund books they believe in – and give fresh ideas that don't fit the traditional mould the chance they deserve.

This book is in your hands because readers made it possible. Everyone who pledged their support is listed below. Join them by visiting unbound.com and supporting a book today.

To Bob Dron, a humble, kind and witty man, who quietly but determinedly championed gender equality in deed and word and laughed every day at Man Who Has It All, from Laura

A Seat at the Table Books, Elk Grove CA
Chance A-R
Amy Abbott
Sandra Abi-Khalil
Christina Ackerman
Amy Adams
Brena (Breeeeena) Adams
Liz Adlam
Kathrin Aegerter
Meg Ahern
Katie Ahmed
David Aitken
Judith Albrecht
Kate Albright-Hanna
Zoe Alderman
Sue Alemann
Syeda Ali
Eva Alisic
Felicity Allen
Nikki Allen
Sionhan Allen
Rob Alley
Nicola Alloway
Everton Zanella Alvarenga
Aurelie Ambal
Angela Amoroso
Vilde Amundsen
Heidi Andersen

Supporters

Alison Anderson
Amy Anderson
Rachel Anderson
Andrea, Lisa, Dölf
Elena Andreassen
Clare Andrews
Susie Andrews
Anna
Fanney Antonsdóttir
Kimberly Anvindr
Kathy Applebaum
Catherine Appleton
Michèle Armbrecht
Michelle Arnold
Laurie Arrowsmith
Sabrina Artus
Anna Ashbarry
Femma Ashraf
Fleur Ashworth
Cat Askew
Charlie Aspinwall
Arlene Astley
Liz Atkins
Joanne Atlee
Ngaire Atmore
Nina Augustsson
Harriet Axbey
James Aylett
Sarah Azouvi
Krista B
Lorena B

Elin Wiberg Baginha
Yul Bahat
Keith Baker
Lisa A Baker
Eleanor Bakker
Emaan Bakshi
Jenny Ball
Sara Balls
Della Bankert
Jennifer Barback
Helen Barclay
Nicola Barn
Jennifer Barron
Brenda Barrows
Angela Barski
Michael Bartlett
Heather Barton
Natalie Barton
Janet Bastiman
Ali Battles
Lima Baum
Rachel Baxter
Vikki Bayman
Irina Bazyrova
Betsy Bearden
Holly Beasley
Sarah Beer
Alison Bell
Emily Bell
George Bell
Tessa Bell

Audrey Benenati
Bettina Benli
Lucie Bennett
Penny Bennett
Maureen Bensa
Veronika Bergmann-
    Prestel
Sylvia Berndt-Bruns
Aadeeba Bhuiyan
Helen Bilton
Jackie Bindon
Chloe Bird
Georgena Bitgood
Kirsten Blackwall
Sally Blandford
Monique Blason
Graham Blenkin
Abigayle Blood
Daniel Boaden
Anca Bobu
Nicole Bodmer
Stacey Bolotin
Hanski Bonanski
Ariane Bonke
Ryan Booher
Japke-d. Bouma
Greg Bowker
John Boyce
Katy Boyce
Andrea Boyd
Christina Bradic

Supporters

Ellen Bradley
Manon Bradley
Mirjam Brands
Pat Brandwood
Sam Bratley
Alicia Ruiz Bravo
Jayne Brayley
R. J. Brewer
Emily Brightwell
Carolyn Brina
Sophie Brookes
Heather Brookfield
Jenni Brooks,
　Katherine Brooks
Charlene Brow
Amanda Brown
Emily Brown
June Brown
Lesley Peebles Brown
Pins Brown
Rachel Brown
Brian Browne
Beth Brumbaugh
Lars Brusell
Matthew Bryant
Monica Buchanan
Molly Buck
Olivia Buis
Floor Buma
Alyssa Burgart
Adriana Burgstaller

Sarah Burnett
Heather Burnham
Erin Burns
Mike Bursell
Lucy Burton
Debs Butler
Kamania Butler
Nicola Butler
Christi Byerly
Tracy Byrne
James Bywater
Emma C.
Libby Cade
Catherine Calder
Lauren Caliolio
Lauren Cameo
Francesca Campalani
Christine Campbell
Irene Campbell
Marcella Campbell
Carla Canfield
Helene Caprani
Wendy Carande
Rusty Carbaugh
Maggie Careless
Simone Carr
Ali Carroll
Anne-Marie Carslaw
Ginny Carter
Margaret Carter
Leslie Carver

Rachel Case
Emily Catmur
Erika Caudle
Gill Cawley
Derek Chambers
Gemma Champ
Christina Chance
Rachel J Chapman
Caroline Charles
Julia Charnock
Aarathi Chellappa
Cindy Chen
Brooke Cheney
Katherine Cheng
Erica Cherup
Kathryn Chew
J Rae Chipera
Stacy Paxson Chittick
Zev Chonoles
John Clairestone
Rebecca Clement
Marjory Clements
Marie-Pierre Cleret
Mieke J. Clincy
Julie Cline
Freyalyn Close-
　Hainsworth
Sten Coeur
Jennifer Cohen
Alexis Cole
Katrina Colistra

Supporters

Kate Collins
Michael Collins
Kevin Conyers
Cheyenne Cook
Sheena MJ Cook
Jennifer Corcoran
Helen Cordery
Carmen Cordiviola
April Cordova
Lisa Corkerry
Rachel Corry
Emilie Cortes
Orlagh Costello
Emma Costelloe
Mike Count
Melinda Cousins
Heidi Coussens
Janae Andrus Cox
Anna Craenen
John Crawford
Lori Crawford
Jennifer Creighton
Nicola Cringean
Sarah Crofts
Laura Crossley
N. Crotty
Tina Crowley
Siobhan Seija
   Cunningham
Kate & BJ Cynics
Theresa D.

Marlena Dachnowicz
Poppy's Daddy
Helen Darke
Anita Das
Michelle Davidson
Ruth Ann Davidson
Debbie Davies
Jade Davies
Nicki Davies
Norah Davies
Leah Davis
Rosie Davis
Penny de Lotz
Milz Dechnik
Thomas DeFreitas
Katie Dehnke
Laura Delahunt
Amy Delcambre
Dudley Denman-Rees
Caroline Dennehy
Kelda Denton
Magdalena
   Derwojedowa
Patric Ffrench Devitt
Heather Devlin
Jamie Dexter
Kinga Di Carlo
Andrea Dottling Dias
   and LJ McEneaney
Floor Dieleman
Lê Song Hoồng Diễm

Michelle Dietz
Daisy Dinwoodie
Karen Disher
Katherine Disney
Carolyn Divish
Brendan Dixon
Ruth Anne Doane
Anne Dobson
Daniel Doherty
Karen Dolan
Phil Dolphin
Amparo Domingo
Elizabeth Donnelly
Josie I Donnelly
Siobhan Donohue
Debbie Donovan
Amelia Donyshery
Patricia Dooley
Nina Dorafschan
Dan Doran
Pat Doran
Diana Dorber
Penny Dordoy
Letizia Dorigo
Alla Doroshkevych
Michèle Dougherty
Christine Doyle
Elaine Doyle
Professor Nancy Doyle
Shirlee Draper
Camilla Drejer

Supporters

Victoria Drew
Laura Dron
Rebekah Drury
Ole-Morten Duesund
Denise Duffield-
 Thomas
Jane Duffus
Fiona Duffy
Emily Duncan
Jane Duncan
Kaye Dunnings
Bronwyn Durand
Philippa Durbin
Tim Dyke
Hannah Dyson
Joe Ebel
Michael Edmunds
Carol Edwards
Kathryn Edwards
Nicole Egan
Francisca Eitjes,
 Diewertje Eitjes
Anke Elbel
Lou Elford
Ashley Elliott
Paula Elliott
Molly Elsegood
Michele Emerson
Liesbeth Vd Enden
Ursula Engels
Erin

Erin, Melina, and
 Kriton Dolias
ES
Amy Eschinger
Amanda Evans
Catherine Evans
Phoebe Evans
Eve Eve (IDJY)
Christine Ewalt
Lauren Exley
Sierra Fairbanks
Elizabeth Falla
 (in memory of)
Laura Faraci
Gabrielle Faraggi
Michele Farmer
Thale Fastvold
Megan Feaver
Betty Feenstra
Zsolt Fejer
Andrea Felde,
 Mashensky
Karen Fellner
Kylie Ferguson
Andrea Santillana
 Fernandez
Charlie Ferrari
Alexander Fick
Sybil Fire
Cecilia Fischer
Liv Fisher

Alanah Fitzgerald
Jodi Fitzpatrick
Sarah Flanagan
Emily Flatt
Stefanie Fleisch
Nick Fletcher
Sharon Burton Fletcher
Alexander Flor
Elaine Ford
Lauren Fotiades
Madeleine Fox
Fr1ee h2ong ko3ng
Amy Franz
Jacquelyn Frith-Crofts
Pavla Mýval Froñková
Mirella Fuchs
Christine Funke
Jamie Gainor
Dr. Karen Zyck
 Galbraith
Chiara Gallese
Nicola Gardham
Stephanie Garis
Manuela Gatto
Jason Genise-Gdula
Lulu Georgiadou
Alex Gessner
Patricia Gestoso
GhoulToast
Joanne Gibson
Katie Giddings

Supporters

Ian Gilson
Rick Giner
Felicia Girdner
Janeen Glenn
Jo Goddard
Maria Godebska
Claire Godwin
Sarah Goffin
Rachel Gollub
Charlie Gombos
Monica Sibaja Gonzalo
Katie Goodall
Ruth Goodbody
Donna Goodley
Max Goodman
Diviya Gorsia
Paige Gottwald
Marylynn Goudy
Jennifer Gourley
Jana Sterling Graber
Beth Graff
Peter C. Gravelle
Liz Grebe
Jen Green
Rachel Green
Emily Greene
Sasha Greene
James Gregory-Monk
Alicia Gresla
Emmaly Gridley
Holly Griffith

Caroline Griffiths
Rebecca Griggs
Nicole Grimm
Saskia Groenewegen
Julia Grover
Elena Groznaya
Marie Grubbs
Jane Guaschi
Sarah Guest
Iveta Gurkovska
Maria Helena
    Gustafsson
Paula Gwinnett
Yasmin Hadi
Claire Hair, CEO
Annika Hallam
Sarah Hallas-Møller
Kate Hames
Anna Hammerschmidt
Sue Hanisch
Julie Hanks
Brian Ch. Hanson
Laura Harder
Katie Jennifer Haring
Shara Jackson Harper
Helen Harris
Larissa Harrison
Jo Haslam
Sian Hatt
Fionna Hawke
Rachel Hazelwood

Hilary Headlee
Angille Heintzman
Callie Heisner
Clara Helfmann
Joshua Heming
Katy Henderson
Marie Herden
Sorcha Herlihy
Kristy and Devon
    Hertzog
Tammy Hervey
Jana Herwig
Andrea Heyting
Gwyneth Hibbett
Amanda Hickling
Femke Hiemstra
Joanna Higginson
Victoria Hill
Briar Hillyard
Helena Hilton
Sharon Hinde
Anne Hingston
Emma Hinson
Inka Hirvanen
Rene Hjetting
Tash Hobbs
Jane Hobson
Jorinde Hoek
Jennifer Hoelscher
Mary Hoffmann
Steph Höhn

Supporters

Rachel Holbeche

Belinda Holdsworth

Mo Holkar

Anne Holland

Jedde Hollewijn

Helen Holmes

Steve Holmes

Nicole Homeier

Paul Homrighausen

Jacki Honig

Louise Honner

Adele Hook

Kate Hook

Janet and Marci
   Hopkins +
   Househusband
   Hoppie

Emma Horgan

Charlotte Horn

Dr Colleen Dorothy
   Horn

Carol Hosokura

Matthew Hothersall

Adam Houghton

Alex Howard

Angie Baker Howard

Cheryl Howard

Chloe Howard

Claudia Howard

Daniel Howard

Sara Howard

Sophie Howarth

Brittany Howell

Cooky Howitt

Sarina Huang

Hansi Hubinger

Jamin Hubner

Chris Hulbert

Amanda Hundt

Jessica Hunt

Silke Huppertz

Caroline Hurr

Nathalia Hurt

Louise Hussey

Fiona Hutchinson

Melanie Hutchinson

Greg Hutt

Kaisu Ikonen

Beccy Ilsley

Rev. Susan Imbs, Ph.D.

Dominic Imrie

In memory of Gerald
   Appleby

Gigi Inara

Miri Inbar

Jeni Indresano

Emma Innes

Glynis Irwin

Lu Ismail

Urška Ivančič

Sherrie Jackson

Torri Jacobus

Elle James

Rebecca James

Changemaker Irene
   Janssen

Ivon Janssen

Jantine

Katie Jantzen

Louise C Jardine

Annie Jarman

Sorscha Jarman

Britta Jarvis

Dyan Jayjack

Helen Jeffries

Jen Dille family

Kim Jennings

Allegra Jensen

Carrie Jensen

Anna Victoria
   Johansen

Andrea Johnson

Dayna Johnson

Emilee Johnson

Glori Headley Johnson

Laura Johnson

Cheryl Johnson-
   Hartwell,

Charlotte Hartwell,

Madeleine Hartwell

Bridgit Johnston

Lydia Joiner

Fi Joines

Supporters

Christine Jones
Devon Jones
Suzanne Jones
Kim Jowitt
John Kaar
KaFo
Ross Kahill
Jordyn Kapperman
Inbal Karo
Sarah Katz
Katrina Kavanagh
Lesley Kay
Melinda Kearly-Pacheco
Wendy Kedzierski
Meredith Keefer
Katie Keeler
Frances Keeton
Jessica Keirns
Angela Kelling
Josefine Kelly
Lorna Kemp
Hannah Kendrick
Jenny Kendrick
Miyuki Kerkhof
Duncan Kerr
Mandy Kerr
Francesca Kerton
Kelli Kessack
Samantha Kilminster
Ali King
Emma King

Josie King
Tina Kinirons
Kelsey Kinney
Lizzy Kirkham
Sanne Klaver
Eva Kles
Katie Klier-Wood
Kristine Klos
Ashley Knight
Lee Knight
Claire Knights
Mel Koetsveld
Paula Kolysher
Maria Kordowicz
Sabina Korpetta
Sven Kosack
Peta Krahn
Katharina Kramer
Helene Kreysa
Kristin, who just adores
 a helpless fella
Sophia Krüger
KSH
Christen Kugener
Valentina Kuhn
Eva Küper
Nicole Kurau-
 Knuefermann
Clare Kutschera
Mel Lacey
Meredith Laing

Dr Leonora Lang
Kyoka Laleuka
Rachel Lamb
Delya Lamerson
Ashe Lan
James Larner
Christina Larson
Laura
Holly Laws
Sophia Lazarou
Hang Le
Keri Le Page
Sarah Leach
Amber Lynn Leavitt
Sandra Lecuyer
Astrid Lee
Emma Lee
Jemma Lee
Trudi Legary
Jan Leitch
Nicole Lemaire
Virginie Lenk
Vera Leonhart
Andrea Lerchl
Laura Leslie
Let's Not Date
Signe Leth
Erin Levin
Tracy Levitt
Alison Lewis
Sara Lichti

Supporters

Juliane Liebsch
Ivana Ligusová
Evangeline Lim
Olivia Lima
Kelli Lincoln
Linda Linda
Carol Ling
Katherine Lingham
Malika Linsner
Laura Liquornik
Ondrej Liska
Katrina Lister
Maggie Little
IMO Anne-Marie
   (Gamma) Littlewood
Lizaroon
Samantha Lloyd
Nikki Lloyd-Brown
Eva Loboda
Errin E Locke
Mistress London
Emma Longland
Tatiana Lopes
Lydia Loriente
Robert Louie
Pavani Lovegood
Gin Lowdean
Alison Lowe
Randi Lucius
Brigitte Colleen Luckett
Luki

Annette Luther
Meghan Lutz
Jeff Lydon
Niamh Lydon
Katrina M
Laure M
Nadja M.
Marian MacAlpin
Nicky MacBeath
Colin MacDonald
Tigger MacGregor
Roderick Mackenzie
Dawn & Michael
   Mackey
Mr Karen Madden
Ottilia Magnusson
Nadia Mahallati
Claire Mahon
Catt** Makin
Donna Malcolm
Traci Mallek
Dr Annetta Mallon
April Mallory
Michelle Malseed
Hedy Manders
Lisa Manske
Meghana Manusanipalli
Sarah Marcotte
Jennifer Marietta
Madeline Marlow
Karen Marriott

David Marshall
Elizabeth Marshall
Laura Marshall
Peter Marshall
Sarah Marshall
Joanna Martignoni
Charlie Martin
Tanisha Martin
Julie Martinez
Steve Mash
Donna Mason
Liberty Mason
Sally Mason
Viki Mason
Sarah Massey
Kusum S. Mathews
Sigh Matsunaga
Julie Mauer
Diana Maurizio
Jon May
Kat Mayes
Mary McAllen
Autumn McAlpin
Shiv McCay
N McConkey
Sarah McCreight
Helen McDiarmid
Kirsty McDowell
Jesika McEvoy
Breanna McGaffin
Fiona McGavin

Supporters

Cat McGill
Pam McGouran
Terri McGuire
David McIlmoyle
Rachel McInnes
Aine McKay
Maura McKay
Juliet McKee
Kate Mckenzie
Sarah Hallion McLachlan
Molly McLaren
Emma McMenamin
Mairead McNeela
Pauline McNeil
Leslie McNeilus
Aidan McQuade
Linda McQuone
Kate Meade
Darren Meer
Alan Meggs
Tatjana Mehlhorn
Francesco Meloni
Ashleigh Melton
Jennifer Mercer
Julie Meredith
A. Merritt
Kristina Meschi
Neva Micheva
Rachael Millar
Elizabeth Miller

Sally Mills
Ruth Milne
Charlotte Minall
Barb Minor
Gabriela Misura
Corinne Mitchell
Maren Mitto
Lisa Moldau
Mark Monahan
Lauren Monson
Jimena Montserrat
Marilyn Moolhuijzen
Jonathan Moore
Katherine Moore
Robyn Moore
Jessie Moorhouse
Lisa Moran
Pippa Morrell
Dr Bev Morris
Marie Morris
Sian Morris
Jane May Morrison
Roxane Mosen
Molly Moth
Charlotte Mountain
Mrs Alexandra Muir
Fiona Muir
Liam F Muldoon
Barbara Mullan
Alexandra Munro
James Munro

Sarah Munt
Cara Murphy
Chrissie Murray
Sean Murray
Teri Myers
Ruth N-G
Imogen Nairn
Kim L. Nalder
Rishabh Nambiar
Carlo Navato
Dr Philip J Naylor
Natalya Nazarevska
Makena Neal
Laura Nebuchadnezzar
Carina Neset
Kay Nevitt
Jennifer Newberry
Sarah Newton
Casey Ngu
Cheska Nicholls
Gary Nicol
Mara Martina Niebuhr
Kellee Nolan
Christoph Nolden
Bonnie Norman
Rachel Norman
Robin Norris
Faith Northcott
Michael Notkin
Ashley Noyd
Beth Nuyens

Supporters

Anja Kjeldaas Nygaard
Sherry Nykiel, M.D.
Jenny O'Gorman
Clare O'Keeffe
Paul O'Neill
Kristy O'Donnell
Samantha O'Kane
Dr. Linda Odenthal-
  Hesse
Szonja Odrovics
Stefanie Oepen
Angelika Ogórkiewicz
Natasha Okeeffe
Angela Olsen
Jeanette Mayland Olsen
Marit Schei Olsen
Emma Olsson
Grace Osborne
Linda Osborne
Empress Ostwald-
  Marquez
Jennifer Oswalt
Abir Othmani
Miranda Otto
Piper Overbaugh
Rose Owen
Simona P
Laura Pacey
Melissa A. Pagonis
Jacquelene Palmer-
  Ambrose

Amy Pandazis
Emily Papel
Francesca Parker
Kate Parker
Steph Parker
Taina Parm
Susan Parrott
Nicky Pascoe
Jeanette Passons
V Patel
Angela Patrick
Rachel Patterson
Dominik Pauli
Jasmin Pauli
Patti Paulson
Jenny Pearcy
Kathryn Pearlman
Emil B. L. Pedersen
Freya Pedley
Jo Peeters
Megan Pelc
Enrico Ercolani Pellini
Jade Penney
Liz Penney-Wroe
Sophie Pepper
Sara Perelmuter
C Peri
Linda Perriton
Eva Peters
Steph Peterson
Petronelise

Thoi Pham
Carly Phelps
Amber Phillips
Carys Phillips
Ladydoctor Jane
  Phillips
Michelle Phillips
Elizabeth Philps
Vania Phitidis
Kathleen Pierce
Charlotte Pike
Jessica Pin
Doris Pinzger
Vanessa Piper
Pauline Archinard
  Piquet
Silke Pizzulli
Sarah Platt
Loretta Platts
Lydia Pluckrose
Brandy Poiry
Annebella Pollen
Polly, Brilliant World
  Leader
Susie Poock
Amy Poole
Iain Douglas Poole
Siriluck Poontong
Sophie Power
Poppy Tyler Prady
Karen Prairie

Supporters

Miriam Price
Christina Priestley
Nick Proellochs
Kate Prouty
Mike Pugh
Karen Purser
Elise Purves
Gisela Qasim
Louise Quick
Kate Quinn
Samantha Radford
Uma Raghavan
Amber Rahim
Michele Rajput
Zsuzsa Rakoskerti
Laura Beatriz Calvo
   Ramos
Amber Rampley
Katie Randall-Stratton
Heather Jean Ransom
Elaine Ray
Meg Ray
Hannah Gabriella Read
Colette Reap
Elizabeth Redpath
Naomi Reeves
Jody Regan
Hannah Renee
Cindy Revol
Kaitlyn Reyes-James
Sonia Reymond

Sara Rhoades
Jules Rhodes
Jennifer Lecocq Rhude
Cindy K Richards
David Richardson
Andrea Richer-Simon
Louise Ridout
Sarah Riedenbauer
Saskia Isabelle Riemke
   and Lorenzo
   Anselmetti
Iacobien Riezebosch
Annalise Roache
Fay Roberts
Jenn Roberts
Xanthe Robertson-
   Sharpe
Damien Robinson
Jane Robinson
Maria Rodgers
Ursula Rodgers
Annica Rofors
Rujuta Roplekar Bance
   & Amit
Malcolm Rose
Sarah Rosendahl
Brianna Rositano
Martine Rostadmo
Hilary Rowland
Sarah Ruiz
Carole Rushall

Catherine Rushall
Sarah Rushall
Chloé Rytz, Men's
   Rights Supporter
Emma S
Melissa S
 S.L.
Amelia Saletan
L. Salinas
Josh Salita
Samuel Saloway-Cooke
Rebecca Samberg
Kaja Sample
Bethany Sanchez
Lilibeth Sanchez
Jesús Martín Sánchez
Anna Sandahl
Amy Sangha
Julia Santomauro
Meredith Savins
Linnea Savisalo
Aleksandra Weder
   Sawicka
Carol Sayles
Andreea Scacioc
Marla Schäfer
G Schauer
Laura Schlögl, BEd.
Evelyne Schmidt
Annelie Schober
Colleen Schoenfeld

Supporters

Birgit Schönfelder
Anna Schoon
Johanna Schuepbach
Kiri Schultz
André Schulz
E. Schweinsberg
Devin Scobie
Jane Ariztegieta Scott
Karen See
Miranda Davis Seed
Torsten Seidel
Mike Sell
Stephanie Sellars
Lucia Sencio
Nadine Senger
Helena Seth-Smith
Daniel Sewell
Joanne Seymour
Cindy Sharman
Ginny Sharp
Joanne Shawcroft
Anna Shea
Sarah Sheard
David Sheehan
Kathryn Shelton
Joey Shepherd
Amy Sheppard
Eliza Sheppard
Paula Sheridan
Justine Sherwood
Karen Sherwood

Juliette Shih
Cambria Siddoway
Michael Sidler
Mirja Siegl
Jen Silverwood
Eleanor Simmons
Lee Ann Simon
Liz Simon
Sigrid Simon
Julie Canavan Simpson
Jennifer Sims
Bethany Singer-Baefsky
Jac Sinnott
Dana Skelly
Jessica Slaght-
    Langworthy
Jody Slater
Gena L. Sluga
Katharine Small
Desrae Smith
Dianne Smith
Emma Smith
Erin Smith
Glenna Smith
Jennifer Smith
Karrie Smith
Lucy Smith
Ros Smith
Sue Ellen Smith
Tina Smith
Victoria Smith

Robert Snedegar
Claerwen Snell
Lauren Sokola
Sara Solvesky
Holly D. Somers
Craig Sommerer
Jennifer Sommers
Astrid Kvam Sorgendal
Lindsey Southerland
Izabel Souza
Hilary Spencer
Dr Renee Spiewak
Emily Householder
    Stacey
Elaine Stafford
Claire Stammars
Philippa Stanford
Danielle Stanley
Deanna Stanley
Jaine Stanway
Lannen Stapleton
Kristin Stavnem
Clarissa Steed
Katharina Stegen
Patrick Stein
Sarina Steinbarth
David Stelling
Kathy Stem
Helen Stephenson
Julie Stephenson
Kushlani Stevenson

Supporters

The Stewards
Sam Stewart
Hazel 'Chief' Stinson
Henrietta Stock
C Stokes
Allison Strachan
Raakhee Stratton
Rachel Stroble
Jeanine Stroop
Vitalija Subota
Elizabeth Sullivan
Q Sumner
Lisa Sutter
Jennifer Sutton
Adam Swallow
Toby Swallow
Helen Tabiner
Nila Tailor
Tess Talbot
Joelle Tamraz
Jodi Tanner
Sharon Tanton
Paula L. Tarrant
Katharine Tatum-
   Krauss
Abby Taylor
Sian Taylor
Libby Tempel
Lorraine Templeton
Jessica Thackaberry
Sarah Thelwall

Alastair Thomas
Charlotte Thomas
Kaleah Thomas
Erin Thompson
Liz Thompson
Nanette Thrush
Tim_G
Anouk Timmer
Reinhard Tlustos
Mike Tobyn
Amanda Toernqvist
Lisa Tomkins
Mat Tomlinson
   #BoyBoss
Joseph Tonna
Megan Tooker
Luke Toop
Lesley Townson
Sarah Trachtenberg
Ju Transcendancing
Evgeniya Travers
Francois Tremblay
Anja E.
   Trenkwalder, MSc
Jane Trobridge
Denise K Tscherner
Stacy Tucker
Rachael Turkington
Sara Turnbull
Michelle Turner
Patrick Turner

Rachel Turner
Annunziata Ugas
Betty Uhlemann
Hanna Umfahrer
Tracey Upex
Sarah Urbanczyk
Helen Urquhart
Niki Vail
Dr. Ilse M. van Bemmel
Alies van Driel
Mathilde Van
   Heereveld
Mareen van Loosen
Saskia van Manen
Esther van
   Rems-Dijkstra
Lenneke van Vliet
Marleen van Zon
Sophie Varlow
Tiina Vartiainen
Vanessa Veiock
Charlie Venn
Mark Vent
Anderwelt Verein
Verity & Zada
Sabina Veronelli
Eline Versluys
Isabelle Vial
Tara Vickery
Celina Vieites
Babs Viejo

Supporters

Eveline Vink
Claartje Vinkenburg
Helena Vlasakova
Katharina Voller
Viola Voltairine
Eleonora Voltolina
Tam Voynick
Clare Wakenshaw
Helen Walden
Karin Waldhauser
Jennifer Walker
Alan Wallace
Hege Rosenlund Wallem
Elaine Walsh
K-Star Walsha
Alison Walters
Emily Walters
Emma Ward
Kenneth Ward
Timothy Ware
Jan Waterfield
Oaive Waters
Craig Watkins
Christine Watson
Clare Watters
Andy Way
Nikki Weekes
Delmer Wells

Lucinda Wells
Tracey Wells
Karin Wendt
Christina C Weston
Jane Weyman
Rebecca Wheaver
Jo Wheeler
Charlotte White
Cassie Stella Whitehead
Penny Whitehouse
Jen Whittle
Joy Whyte
Susan E. Wigget
Rosemarie Wilde
Meggie Wilhoite
Trish Wilkins
Suzanne Wilkinson
Patricia Williams
Susan Williams
Tricia Williams
Fiona Willmott
Dayna Willms
Cathryn Anwyl Wills
Lynette Willsey-Schmidt
Kerry Wilson
Melissa Wilson
Christine Winkler
Camilla Winqvist

Emily Winslow
Laura Winter
Lisa Wirth
Wivine
LJ Wms
Charlotte Wolf
Nadine Wolf
Kat Wood
Sara Wood-Gates
Jody Woodbridge
Lydia Woodland
Skye Woodrum
Ioonah Woods
Robert Woods
Susie Worley
Amber Wozniak
Liz Wray
Robert Wright
Nicola Wunderlich
Jessica Yaeger
Desiree Yap
Lucy Yeomans
Jasper Yoo
April Young
George Zahora
Christian Zangl
Gretchen Zimmerman
Erna Zodi